It's Damn Near Erotic When I Think About It

My Journey To Becoming Aware And Staying Aware

GAMINA OLIVER

CONTENTS

Introduction

I decided to write this book because I wanted to share many personal experiences, thoughts, and philosophies about my encounters on my journey to self-awareness through the last twenty-five years of my life. This book is based on an actual seminar presented in front of a live audience. Although this story is about my self-awareness, it has something everyone from all walks of life can relate to. Warning, it also contains some dramatic language. As you read you will see that we all share some very basic commonalties. The interpersonal strengths that I learned in the schoolhouse of life, I really thought that I stumbled onto them by mistake, because the reality of them all was extraordinary and beyond my beliefs. However, with every religious experience, phenomena I witnessed, or scientific encounter, I got stronger and stronger in my beliefs. I began seeing things differently because there was truly more to observe. During my journey I would share with others the awakenings these experiences revealed to me, and the more people I shared with, the more people I found had extraordinary experiences of their own to share. You too can experience these things as I have; you just have to open your minds to see the clues. For me, at times, it was like a blinker signaling me which way to turn at the next corner. Other times it was like the "no pressure" rule; if you have done all your prep work before hand then you would reach your desired outcome. One of my major discoveries on this journey is that "things literally do fall in your lap", it's just a matter of being in the right place at the right time, and being in the state of acceptance because the windows of opportunity do open and close around you. I believe I have witnessed these happenings by being on the right path.

PART 1

The Water Is Cold

HEY You All; ahhhh—ahhhh—ahhh! Come on, come on! Give me a few more seconds. Ahhhh—ahhh! This water is cold! Ahhhh—ahhhh—5, 4, 3, 2, 1, cut it off! That water is cold as hell this morning! But in my case it's cold each and every morning. That was my cold shower treatment that I use to get my head right when I think about "IT" in a way that I'm not suppose to be thinking about "IT"! Now I know you think I'm just another black businesswoman who's lost her mind from the pressure of it all - wait, wait, wait! Let me put the back of my hand on my forehead and get in the "I think I'm going to faint" pose. Ha, Ha, Haaaaa - that's funny. Now, I can't lie, some of the things that I've witnessed could use an interpreter, because I just don't quite know how to explain some of "IT".

I know that some of you may be thinking what is "IT"? "IT" is the eroticism of my journey in all its glory. Some mornings I can't control the overwhelming bliss that overcomes me when I think of the joy that fills my heart, the warmth that fills my loins, and the feeling of love that heightens my emotions. I become speechless in the rapture of "IT" all.

What could give me such a feeling that can't be described any other way? How about for one the feeling of hope - desire. Let me try to explain to you the experiences I've had with the outcome of hope. Hope for me is the foundation for believing. Once I have identified a need or want in my life, I will it into existence starting with hope. And with that hope, I dig deep within myself and grasp onto the feeling that promotes the desire to achieve an outcome. Then I focus all my energy to that outcome. I say to myself, "I can do this, and I will". Now don't get me wrong, it took a little practice, but this works for me.

Have you thought about your feelings of hope? Do they have all of your dreams and realities embodied in this very emotional feeling? Have you questioned your ability to have hope or have you just given up? Did you wake up this morning and decide that you have nothing to hope or dream for - so the hell with it?

Listen, you're not the only one who has these thoughts and you won't be the last one either. We are so human sometimes we forget to make ourselves push pass simple limitations that we've grown accustomed to in our day-to-day life style.   We get in to a routine too quickly and we don't exercise the "what if" anymore; "what if I took a little more time"; "what I did it a different way"; or "what if I succeed, then what will I do"? What...are we afraid to do things differently because it may challenge us to do better for ourselves? That's like saying, "I'm afraid to have hope...things may get better for me?" Is that such a bad thing? You may have to work a little harder at accomplishing your goal. Aaahhh...is that it? You don't want to work too hard; you don't have the time; or you can't afford it. Big dreams come with big price tags. First of all let me begin by saying you just wasted a lot of positive energy on the "I don'ts" and the "I cant's".

Now lets talk about the reality of hope. False hope is when you say, "I hope I win the million dollar *Lotto*", but you don't play every day. This is not the hope I am talking about.

A good example of what I mean happened recently while I was parked in front of the empty house next door to mine and I noticed a man sitting on a porch. I got out of the car and we exchanged hellos. He spoke up and told me not to be alarmed that he was sitting on the porch, he used to live there.

I knew the house was for sale and asked if he was trying to buy the house? He replied, "I wish I could". He said that he wasn't able to purchase the house, but he had talked to several family members with hope that one or more of them would get together and buy the house so that it would stay in the family.

I could see the look of desperation on his face and hear it in his voice. When I asked if he knew people are interested in purchasing the house, he said yes, that's why he's been reaching out to family members. Then he said he was looking for work and if I or someone I knew needed sidewalk concrete repair work done he was available. I asked if he poured slabs for decks and he asked if I could show him where I wanted it. He got up from the porch of his previous residence - walked down the stairs - stopped and looked back at the porch.

I asked him what was wrong? He said, I guess my bible should be okay if I leave it on the porch. Then he turned and walked out of the gate and said, "well if they do take it, I hope it's because they need it like I do right now." This man is holding on to the hope that maybe his family will look pass his unfortunate situation and character, and listen to what he said about keeping the house in the family; he is holding on to the reality of hope.

 The same principle applies to any desire that you may have all you need to start with is hope. Just by saying to yourself, "I can do it, and I will", you are willing your hopes into existence." Just visualize what it is you are hoping for, and give that hope the positive energy it needs to accomplish each step toward your goal. Nothing can stop you from achieving your desires and dreams but you.

You will hear that again throughout this book because that is the biggest challenge we have today. We can't get pass our own idiosyncrasies to better ourselves. Why can't we do the simplest things better just to please ourselves. You've heard of it before - "self gratification". To me this means, to challenge myself; "I dare me to do better for me...to satisfy me", breaking that old habit of always putting someone else's pleasure before mine.

Where do you start? With your inner strengths; where do you think inner strength comes from - positive reinforcements. We can get this from other people such as role models. Being around strong role models can give us that much needed inspiration. But what if you don't have any role models in your mist? Where will you go to find them, or better yet, how will you be able to develop your own inner strengths you need to succeed as the person you want to be? Before we embark on this journey let me give you something to think about along the way...when it is said and done you are your biggest fan and supporter. Therefore it's time for you to reach within yourself and find your inner strengths. You need to become your own positive role model. How?...began by capitalizing on what you are good at. For example, if you are good at cooking...then you have the strength to nurture. Everyone has something that they excel at you just have to stop sabotaging yourself by thinking you're not good at anything, or not good enough at any one thing. And if you are limiting yourself by thinking, "oh poor me I have been through so much I can't think straight". Its time to get over it! This is what hope can do for you. After you cry, kick and scream, and get all the negative energy out of your system, you need to decide what you need to do next to help yourself, and then do it.

If you need to partner with someone to help you get started, then do so and talk to him or her about what you're trying to do. That person could be a minister or other spiritual leader, a therapist, a community leader, or someone you know that has succeeded in what you are trying to do. Now I know that many people do not have the money or benefits for a visit to a therapist. However, ministers are leaders in the community that are very accessible.

Although people go to church for various reasons, I believe the main reasons is hope. Now we all know the minister will try to get people to join the church, that's not a bad thing...that's what they are supposed to do. We also know that the ministers expect to get paid for the job. How? By having people attend church services and supporting church functions. We all know that there are those people that will seek the help of the church, then repay their debt to their satisfaction, then stop going to church until they are in need again. You know who you are, so don't get mad at me I'm just keeping it real. But remember the business of the church does need money to pay the bills, so when you can give money support the church. Now, I am not trying to take you all to church, I just needed to get my plug in. I know that everyone's "Higher Power" does not follow the same religious or spiritual path that mine do so substitute your own beliefs where needed. I am not trying to convert you but I am trying to get you to open you mines and become aware of what's in front of you. Keep in mind that we are talking about hope and strength, which is the fabric of faith. In order to have hope you must have faith – in your self.

For those of you that have attended a church service, how do you feel after you leave? Don't you just want to burst from the joy you feel? You are filled with so much hope that your emotional cup runneth over. Isn't it such an amazing feeling? You feel so full that tears can fill your eyes and run down your face in a constant stream. Your heart will beat strong like the drums in Africa. It can take your breath away like the wind and render you absolutely speechless at the same time. The blood in your veins will heat up and flow through your body like a rapid river. You will want to scream but can't. You will want to run but can't. As you stand still paralyzed from the overwhelming emotion, your mind will elevate you to a place that's so still with peace, it's damn near erotic when you think about it.

What I Do Know

WHAT I do know is this; its possible that we all have experienced some small or large phenomenon that we just can't explain. For instance, do you know why a grown woman just took a one-minute cold shower? Ha,Ha,Haaaa!

Now let me "back that *thang* up" and tell you what happened to me to bring me to this state of mind. The experience was so incredible it took me a couple of weeks to realize that my feet were still planted firmly on the ground, but I had to look down to check anyway, just to be sure. What I was feeling was similar to that of an out of body experience.

Let me begin by telling you a little about myself before my journey began. I was a person who wanted to be defined as an individual. I wanted people to view me as a person of good character, great personality and just plain old down-to-earth; and anyone who knew me couldn't say that I was a person of pretense. But more than that I wanted to be thought of as "normal"...whatever the hell that's supposed to mean. So, I could say that my journey began when I was off in search of this person I wanted to become when I "grew up" *so-to-speak*.

Well, I grew up, and I do mean GREW UP, in a Baptist church - so you can see where my attachment to the church comes from. My uncle was the Minister of the church and therefore I was part of the family labor pool that supported and ran the church. In short, the members of the congregation had the option to show up for church on Sunday...I didn't! The members had the option to show up for choir rehearsal... I didn't! The members had the option to show up for Bible studies, "all together now"... I DIDN'T!

My daily activities consisted of going to school, playing sports, and going to church, and not necessarily in that order! The things I remember most about school were spirit week, basketball, and astrology. Yes!...I said astrology and I know that I am not the only one here that had their head in the stars during high school.

But seriously, astrology was a great conversation starter. Everyone you talked to wanted to know, "what's your sign"? And with my upbringing in the church it was only natural that I grabbed a hold of this astrology thing, you know, with the stars, moon, heaven and all...could I get "any closer" to God? I know I'm not the only one that has gone *"there"* on occasion too, and some of us still do.

Anyway I became very interested in astrology and reading the daily horoscope and asking, "what's your sign", just wasn't satisfying the many questions that I had. Questions such as why people with the same astrology sign that I have don't act like me, or I like them?

My astrology sign is *Pisces*. I have worked, played, and associated with several men and women who were also born under the sign of *Pisces*, and oddly enough I didn't behave like any of them, according to the horoscope. So, I said to myself - "Self...why don't you act like that, you're a *Pisces*?" I thought I was just a "normal" *Pisces,* not a "Special Ed" Pisces. Which still wasn't good enough to answer my questions.

Remember I am that person trying to find my own individuality, so I was glad that I was different, but I needed to find out why. So my happy little ass began researching other areas of astrology.

And what many areas does astrology have! And would you believe that there are charts and other evidence to back up everything!!! Two charts that I found very interesting were the natal chart and the numerology chart.

The natal chart is a chart that is drawn for you using many variables that will give you the understanding of yourself. The numerology chart uses numbers to analyze things about you. In both cases you will be able to use these charts as a guide to plan your life and maximize your full potential.

While studying these charts I learned that our destiny can be determined according to the time of our birth. Now wait just a minute y'all...did I, or did I not stumble onto some reality type of shit? Oh, and it got even better when I got to the sections that tells you about what's going on with the positioning of the moon, sun, and planets at the time of your birth. And it was during one of my studies, I remembered when I was a teenager, I overheard some people talking about this very subject on a school trip to the planetarium.

You know how you overhear people talking about certain topics, and after listening to a little bit of the conversation you decide if you want to continue to eavesdrop or not? I decided not to continue listening because I thought they were "full of it". Well, I was having one of those trips down memory lane while reading about these charts.

So, I had to check myself again; I said, "Self...are you going to believe any of the shit you just read or are you going to walk away... again?" I don't know if I went into a daydream or had a psychosis episode but all kind of things started running through my mind. For example, I could hear my uncle ministering affirmations from the Bible. I remembered a particular sermon he delivered during one Sunday morning service. The message stated, "You are here for a reason." Of course everything he said that day made me feel as if he was talking directly to me. In my church everybody's mama would tell me the same thing; "It doesn't matter what day you show up in church there's a message for you, and it always seems to come out of the Ministers mouth right when you need it." Y'all, they were right about that!

Anyway after that moment of revelation about the charts my interest was really peaked, and I continued researching over the next several years. I crossed all kinds of thresholds from comparative religions to psychic beliefs, herbal healing to gemstone therapy, chakras, astro-projecting, and the yin and yang! Now, I have to be honest with you, some of these findings went better with a spiked beverage because they were just too overwhelming.

I know that I am not the only one that has ventured so far into these teachings. Some may have taken the "Nestea Plunge" and studied all at once like I did, or some of you may have absorbed bits-and-pieces as you've grown. Many of you are right where I am. Don't feel bad, hell I thought I was crazy just for indulging in all the stuff that I was reading. For those of you that are not familiar with any of these practices, I will continue to mention them briefly as we go along.

So as you can imagine I just about fell over when I realized that I had been right as a teenager...there is a lot more to us than just our birth sign. As far as I can tell we are born under three astrology signs - not just one!!! We are governed by the arrangement of planets and cosmic order. The natal chart shows the position of planets and astrological houses at the time of your birth. The natal chart also reveals natural characteristics, strengths, and weakness.

As referenced by several astrology charts, we are born into strengths and weaknesses. This is why it's so important to know your self, keeping in mind that you may have inherited some of the strengths and weaknesses of your parents. Remember you are in charge of your destiny and therefore you can capitalize on your strengths and work at overcoming your weaknesses. So, don't keep blaming your parents for your weaknesses because you can change them.

What's important to me about the natal chart is that it clearly tells you what jobs or careers that naturally fit your life. For those of you that are still struggling with career choices, having a natal drawn up for you may be a good place to start. Along with other elements, the chart uses the positioning of the moon and the sun, and the alignment of the planetary houses at the time of your birth to determine, influence and enhance your personality, creativity, self-expression and self-identity as referenced by many astrologers.

This, I discovered, is why I don't act like a typical "Pisces". I have more Sagittarius characteristics and Scorpio attributes added to my strengths. I found that my love to work and to be successful was in my chart. I work hard at balancing career with my strong sense of family. Trust me, I have lost relationships not knowing the formula to this balance.

But once I learned how to make conscious changes that affect my energy, physical ailments, friends, conflicts, business and investments, I must admit, I've had success by becoming aware of my self. How deep is that! Are you all still with me? I don't want to lose anyone. And don't think I am crazy just yet, I still have more to explain before you send the jury out.

The more knowledge I gained the more I wanted to know, and so much more was revealed to me including the yin and yang principles and Feng Shui. Both practices deal with the flow of your life-energy within your immediate surroundings, both inside and outside of your home.

Both of these practices also involve the incorporation of many elements including wood, fire, metal, earth, and water as they work together to produce harmony. Feng shui deals with the direction and the placement of the elements in your space to ensure a constant flow of positive energy. Yin and yang deals with the equal balance of the universe as a whole. Where one falls short of its intended purpose the other kicks in to ensure the proper balance is always kept.

For some of you I know what I have mentioned here is a lot to absorb and it definitely is a lot to comprehend, but I wanted to mention some tools that may assist you in your studies of self. Therefore I encourage you to research some or all of what was mentioned here as it pertains to you.

There are many more idealisms out there that I did not mention but remember this book is about my journey to self awareness, so what I have mentioned is what I have studied. Also realize that you do not have to adopt any one practice, but choose what works for you out of the each one you discover.

If you truly want to know about life and how all the little quirks and crazies move you in and out of episodes a moment at a time, start reading about anything that affects your religion, behavior, or psyche—you will freak out.

The good news is you will have a better understanding of chaos and karma. In a sense, chaos arranges or directs the elements of a situation to produce a desired effect, and karma is all about cause and effect. People, don't let the fancy words fool you. You must "reap what you sew"; you have to pay for your wrong doings one way or another and it could be now or later, but you will pay.

Now, if you understand the theory behind chaos and karma you can relate that to the good and bad, or positive and negative energy.

Depending on what part of the world you grew up in, that translates into many different names. But those of us that believe in a heaven and hell, knows there is a greater force.

So, I'm sitting there literally mind-tripping about all of the information that I've consumed and started putting together some interesting pieces of the many puzzles in life, but particularly how it applied to my life.

What I didn't realize was that while reading, studying, and researching all of the different subject matters, and comparing pros and cons from many authors, researchers, religious leaders, philosophers, archeologist, history books and others, I became more aware. I became more sensitive to my surroundings. In a sense, I woke up my psyche.

Ten years later, I realize I'm a grown woman walking around with a quartz crystal in my pocket on a daily basis. I may take off a day or two from exercising or eating right, but my crystal stays in my pocket, purse, coat, or car. I can't turn this off and I can't walk away from it.

Why am I walking around with a crystal in my pocket? Did you know that the quartz crystal has many healing properties as stated in gemology books? If fact, I have found it to be great for headaches. In my studies, I learned that by carrying the quartz crystal you send a signal into the ethers (the universe) and receive a signal from the ethers.

Remember, "Ask and you shall receive." But just like the crystal, there are other things that I just can't pass up, such as the subject matters of global weather conditions, anything on the evolution of the planet, or discoveries in the solar system.

I lived in Phoenix, Arizona for a short time and while I was there I had an opportunity to visit the mountains. Although the sun was cooking me from the inside out, I couldn't miss out on a chance to go to a part of Four Peaks Mountain and see gemstones that formed there.

Not just any gemstone, but the purple and white amethyst. *** You have to look for a clear purple one in other regions.*** The effects of being on that mountain were so incredible. I felt the energy from the gemstones being absorbed by my body, and I sat down for a while to take it in. The feeling was very calming and peaceful. I felt as if I was bonding with this energy that passed through me in a magnetic but settle way.

Unfortunately I had to leave Phoenix because I couldn't find work there and the heat was unbearable, but boy did I love those mountains. There were job opportunities in Denver, CO, so, we packed up the car and the kids and left. As you get close to Denver, the first real vision that captivates you is the mountains. I couldn't believe how beautiful they were.

A few days later, I finally got an opportunity to take a drive and sight see. I got out the car and walked down a path to a scenic area. About ten minutes into the walk, it happened again just like in Phoenix, that overwhelming feeling of energy being absorb by my body. I sat down for a minute and it consumed me. I literally felt like I had been swallowed hold.

After a while, I was released as if I stood up out of a tub of hot bath water. I felt like I had been de-magnetized. I know now, that I was having an epiphany, a moment of sudden revelation or insight.

I had been traveling, designing and selling clothes, and modeling in the tri-states for about two years. More money passed through my hands then I care to remember - since I spent it living very well. So, when I moved there my first thought was, "what is it about this place and why does this feel so different?"

I've never traveled to Denver or Phoenix before so those states weren't on my radar. I had no interest in these states because they did not pertain to my career at the time. I have flown passed them or had a layover on my way to California, but that was all.

So quite naturally I am kind of baffled, because everyday I wake up, I'm experiencing this feeling that I've never felt before and It's running through my body and holding my thoughts constantly. I was staying with friends temporarily until I could find a job and a place to stay. However during this time the only thought I'm having is how am I going to shake this feeling. I remember thinking it will pass... it's just because I'm in a new city and state in a different part of the country. I'm probably just having an adjustment period.

It was the fifth day since I've arrived in Denver; I was up early as usual and out of the apartment to find a job. The economy was starving for workers in Denver and I found a job very quick. I go into a Honda dealership with a help wanted sign. Praise God! They hired me that day and the next day I'm working hard trying to prove myself. The Supervisor walked up to me while I was detailing a car and told me, I was supposed to go to lunch two hours ago, comments on how good of a job I'm doing and kicks me out the shop for an hour.

I had a packed lunch, so I jumped in my car, a 1976 Buick Century I called Old Faithful since it got me from Phoenix to Denver and only broke down once. A rubber plug came off from over heating, but the tow driver gave us a replacement, filled Old Faithful up with a water and antifreeze mixture and we were back on the road in two hours.

So, I'm at lunch driving down the street and looking around at all the help wanted signs. I thought to my self; self, you really need to make as much money as you can so that you can get an apartment as soon as possible.

Back then you could ask friends or family to let you crash at their house for a few weeks until you found work and place to stay. But I was taught that if you asked for help and you were blessed to receive it, you should be up at the crack of blue sky doing what you needed to do to handle your business. Don't even get me started on these lazy kids being raised today!

Anyway, before my lunch break was over I had stopped at a couple of stores on the same street and put in applications for part time jobs. I would get off work at Honda and run by the apartment where I was staying with friends, pick up my partner and the kids and go looking for our own place to stay.

There were two areas we liked that was recommended by our friends, and wouldn't you know, there was a gas station across the street from the apartment complex of our first choice with a help wanted sign in the window. Again, as I was taught, I did not put off what can be done today until tomorrow.

So we pulled into the station and I got a little gas, and when I went in to pay for it I asked for two applications. Yep...we made it a family outing, we let the kids out to run around by a near by car wash while my partner and I filled out the applications.

The next day we were double dipping in glory. The apartment management accepted our applications and the gas station hired my partner full time and me part time. Within one week we had three jobs and an apartment! We couldn't move into our apartment until the end of the month, and the kids needed a babysitter since they were too young to care for themselves.

But this was not a problem...one of our friends that we were staying with kept an eye on the kids while we did the work thing. By the end of the month we had our move-in money, plus a little extra that we gave our friends for letting us crash at their place. We grabbed our furniture out of storage and moved in our very own apartment.

Now maybe you are thinking what I'm thinking...and wondering if that strange feeling I was experiencing ever went away? Actually no, in fact it changed into something that can be associated with a super energy drink. I felt like I had the energy of ten athletic women all riding the same bike.

I had to check my self from time to time because my energy level was so high it was off the charts. Now keep in mind that I've never been to this part of the country before and have no idea why I've turned into the superwoman I have become. That's not all, I stayed on this high-energy cycle for fourteen years but it didn't take me that long to go read about what was happening to me.

I believe there is an energy that surrounds us, it's everywhere; this energy grounds us to the earth and expands our minds so we can absorb the universal phenomena and all it's glory. You have to be still to feel its existence. But it is alive.

You remember the saying, "you are here for a reason." Apparently I was suppose to be right where I was, surrounded by mountains. Not because their just mountains with all their beauty, but because of the natural energy that mountains contributed to my grounding.

Obviously it was a time in my life that I needed to be grounded...to be still for a while. It was then that I began to realize that everything I touched turned into something very positive. It was like having a tree full of fruit in its season. I was living through being blessed, and it didn't stop for fourteen years. I would wake up laughing sometimes from the shear joy that I felt. And I projected that joy, I was terrified to do anything wrong, or let anyone near me that wasn't acting right.

You talk about cleaning your house of negative thinking people or wrong-doer's. Y'all, I started checking everybody I came in contact with see if I could see or feel the God in them. My natural intuitive meter was running twenty-four hours a day, seven days a week. I was not going to let anyone mess this up for me and I wasn't going to mess it up for myself.

I recognized the fact that I was exactly where I was supposed to be. I thought of what my elders would say; my great grandmother Lula, grandmother Julia, aunt Anna and uncle Tim; what words would they have said to enlighten me at this crossroad in my life, then it came to me; "God takes care of old people, children, and fools".

I didn't understand at first, I thought even in their death…"they got jokes". But on a routine drive to work one day, the 23rd Psalms rolled out my mouth as easy as the air I breathe as it often does, especially after I recognized the clairvoyance of what God has blessed me with…"I am the fool". Why am I the fool?

Sometimes, God has a way of directing us the right way on our journey through life by making us see things differently

Remember I was overwhelmed by my first contact with the mountains in Phoenix, but I wasn't ready, I wasn't in the state of acceptance. Although the mountains in Denver held me in its grasp, I wasn't afraid because I always felt that I was free to go whenever I chose.

Although I was blinded by my passion of making money, I stayed around long enough to absorb the real message…I am a part of something wonderful. It was then that I came in to my state of acceptance.

As I continued to grow in spirit through meditation, I realized that my spirituality had expanded to include the material I've studied instead of conflict with my religious beliefs. It also made me realized that I have two parts of my being. Some of us struggle every day to maintain balance between our bodies and our animal instinct. To me this means we can be as ignorant as we want to be. Ignorance comes in all sizes, shapes, colors and nationalities. I have to control my self and I worked on me. I use the gemstones to help direct my energy inward. I use meditation to focus that inward energy within my charkas so I can exhale the negative energy that raises within me from the stress of dealing with people and their surprising behaviors.

I work hard at not letting others poor behavior, rub off on me. But sometimes, the strength I need to control the animal nature within me drains me of my energy. Therefore, I use my studies to rejuvenate not only my body, but my mind and spirit. This has been the blessing of being aware. When you need to replenish yourself, you know what resources you can use to immediately restore your positive energy.

That's why I was able to identify my natural direction as a business manager and developed this skill by volunteering for manager training and leadership programs. I was able to walk right into a career that fits me perfectly. I became aware of what worked and what didn't within my professional and personal environments. If I tried something and it just didn't feel quite right, I left it along. I tried not to confuse friction with missed opportunities.

This part was challenging. In my opinion, friction is trying to force something that doesn't fit your capabilities eighty percent or better. You all know this but do to your current situations, or in desperation, you waste a lot of time and energy on something that isn't right for you in the first place. It's like working against your self.

Most of us know not to waist valuable time beating on a door where our chances of success aren't good. Find your area of expertise and focus your energy there. This is where you put your best foot forward. Those people that help themselves by knocking on doors where their experience is needed eighty percent knows this increases their chances.

Let's not get this confused with not trying hard enough to obtain something or some position that we want. You have to collect the ingredients to make the meal first. Don't just sit back and wish you had something, but yet don't contribute any effort toward receiving it. Now you're wasting your own time.

I'm quite aware that you have the right to waste your own time the way you want to, but you may be setting yourself up to become a "hater". Because you didn't have the drive or desire to get up and obtain the life style you wanted, your lack of ambition increased your "hate" for the people that successfully obtained the life style they have. Let's go there for a minute.

I came from a family where "can't" just wasn't in the vocabulary. If it slipped out your mouth someone within listening range was quick to correct you in a very "political" manner. They would say…" Don't say can't honey. You can do anything you put your mind to". How true they were.

When I reflect back on my life, I've driven cars that I wanted to drive and lived in houses in the suburbs I wanted to live in. I've traveled to places I wanted to travel to thus far and I have always had two successful careers.

My second career in entertainment included writing screenplays for cinema movies, creating and coordinating music video scenes. A promotional talent coordinator for festivals, commercials, local TV shows, music video's, concerts and movie extra's. A personal manager and image consultant for models, actors, R&B and jazz vocalist, rappers and hip-hop artists contracted for local studio and state venues.

I came from a musically incline family. I was always more interested with organizing what we were trying to do more than playing the instruments in front of me. But I tried anyway. At some point you have to realized, that you have the talent to play an instrument or not. So organizing talent shows became my calling.

I started helping with school talent shows then coordinating youth dance groups and bands for city festivals and a movie in Michigan. However, when I moved to Denver, I started working with music industry promoters that coordinated talent for opening acts of concerts and promotional events for clothing sponsors.

I started managing and being an image consultant for artist working in the music studio on their da'beau CDs, demos for A&R reps from Polygram and Universal music labels and two local TV shows.

I didn't want to stray away from writing screenplays for cinema movies, so in between working on getting promoted at my job, coordinating talent and promoting and managing a full of music artists, I continued to write one screenplay, then another until I had three completed movie scripts. So I started looking for an agent. This was tougher then I thought it would be. But I did find a producer that was willing to let hang out and learn more about the movie industry.

I stuck to him like a coat of paint. Remember, I have discovered my talent is in organizing and coordinating. So no acting for me; I wanted to learn the job of the producer.

What was amazing to discover was the fact that this natural ability to be a manager helped me understand the job of the producer fast. The producer's job is to manage the film shooting process from every assistant, actor, caterer, location, accommodations, all paperwork, legalities and finances involved with starting and completing the film.

I started networking with movie producers in New York and Chicago for more experience. I was ready to move ahead with my film projects. I now knew that my chances of producing my films would happen faster as an independent film producer as opposed to working for an established film company. This wait could be eternal as they don't take new writers or producers with out referrals or so many accredited films. You can't get an accredited film because you can't get anyone to give you a chance.

Yeah; I was out of there and dealing with SAG in Chicago on becoming an independent film producer. After I moved there I attended several training seminars while collecting people already connected to the industry so when I'm ready to produce my first independent film I now have references.

I Have seen the return on my time invested on my self and in my careers from taking advantage of the knowledge I've studied which has taught me to be aware by maintaining and focusing my positive energy and following the opportunities made available to me.

I put the time in and tested this idealism according to my natal and numerology charts complete with the planetary alignment combined with the house of time characteristics and personalities.

I became a walking test subject for years. The amazing thing is that I was able to decipher the information under a theory or ideology. I had to keep in mind what I was trying to accomplish in order to know what category I would be dealing with. I would research the ideology and apply its techniques or watch for the signs of opportunity to fulfill my objectives. I had to start being aware of the signs that lead to the answers of the metaphysical, theological, scientific and universal phenomena's. I knew when to leap with both feet or lay back and let certain negative energy pass. I didn't do anything to upset the balance in my life.

There's something to say for all that I have seen and accomplished. But, as sure as your birth is stamped by time, your path is designed for you. It doesn't mean that every one is going to be rich, famous, smart, tall, attractive or any of the superficial things we wish for. It seems that everyone's path could have them doing just what they're suppose to be doing today. And if you're blessed with a special gift or talent, you were born with it. You may have enhanced it through practicing or some form of training, but it appears that you were born with it.

So for those that chose to fall off or turn off their path, they could have missed out on their life just as it was meant to be. Some of us re-cooperate from some of life's pitfalls and ugly challenges they may come our way. But clearly some of us cannot.

If you are one of the people that make your way back on to your natural path of life, keep your head up and your eyes forward. Your blessings are still yet to come. Don't bog your self down by becoming jealous and envious of people. Be grateful for what is given to you by walking on the right path. Your blessings will be upgraded as you make your way up the path.

Both of my parents are alive as well as all of my siblings. I feel so blessed I can only think of my life. I don't need to be worried about what someone else has.

I have never been known for being a jealous or envious person. That could be because I'm guilty of working too much. Every thing has its gives and takes right. But, to sit around complaining about something I don't have or want, is not me.

I have moved into a duplex across town because my partner and I have gone our separate ways. I have a new job thanks to a lead from a friend of a friend and I started managing and promoting a female R&B vocalist who can stop you and make you look for the beautiful sound of her voice as she sang a cappella walking through the mall one day. I have a new love interest and things are going well thus far.

I am working on learning the transportation industry because it's new to me but it fits me like a glove. Although my charts noted a positive career change I still look for a feeling from a company. That feeling tells me if I'm going to be there long or short term. Sometimes, it's just a stepping-stone that leads me to the next step. But I had a good feeling about my decision.

A few months went by and I got a new neighbor moving in next door. I introduced my self before leaving for work one day. I don't ask people to many questions when I first meet them but I am checking them out as often as I can until I get to know them better.

I was returning home from work one night and I over heard my neighbor commenting about my car and my job. I wore a company shirt so it was obvious that I worked for a nationwide transportation company.

I over heard her say, " she probably think she somebody because she got that good job and a nice car." This was funny to me because a job or car should not define who you are as a person, they're just apart of your status. Now, I had to get to know them.

I was home on the weekend and saw them pull into the driveway. I went out side and spoke to them and asked them if they were settled in and what the thought about the neighborhood. After they replied I asked them what they did for a living, where they use to live, did they have family living in town and a host of other questions that kept them talking and laughing with me for about an hour.

By the time they went in the house, they were telling me how down to earth I was and they were glad to have chatted with me.

Sometimes I have to get rid of people's assumptions of who they think I am by sharing a little bit of who I am with them.

If it bothers you so much that your neighbor has a nice car or house, that you have deemed better then yours, get up and go get you a better car or that house. Now, if your appetite is bigger than your wallet, you may have to work two, threes jobs, but you can have whatever you can afford.

When I see a friend or family with a car that I like, I jump on the passenger side or ask for the keys, because either way I'm going for a ride. I usually tell them…"come on, let's go, so I can enjoy your car with you". When a friend or family member purchase a new house they always have a cookout so their loved ones can come over and enjoy one another while celebrating the accomplishments of that family. Their hard work, prayers, and "will" to achieve their goals have paid off.

I don't understand how people have so much time to hate or be jealous of what someone else has worked hard to obtain. This means people still have way too much time on their hands when they need to be out there working on a plan to get what they want out of life. So, put down the drama and pick up your life; you can do this!

Every time someone complimented me on my positive attitude, I said thank you. For me, It's a great filling to have someone recognize that I have a good attitude. I know that everyone doesn't come with a good attitude and it's not something you can just run out to the super market and pick up.

I said earlier that you have to have the right ingredients to make the meal. The ingredients started with me having a good attitude. You would not believe how many doors you can open with just a good attitude and a smile.

I've interviewed some people with wonderful attitudes. They may or may not be very polished and that's all right with me. But in my heart I know they will give there best efforts. I have had people tell me, "I will give my best. I don't know if my best is good enough for you but your getting my best all the same." I respect that in a person. We are not all things to all people, if you've figured that out, then you'll have another ingredient to go with that meal.

If your best is not enough for what you're doing, you still have two options. You can find out what it takes to take yourself to the level of expertise their looking for or you can go somewhere that can use the expertise you have now. If you chose to step up your knowledge so you can increase your level of experience and go back as a contender for that job you didn't qualify for six months ago, then by all means, go do the damn thing. There are no rules in the life of goals and accomplishments. You can keep going until you are satisfied with yourself. That would be taking the initiative and adding another ingredient to the meal.

What about our passage? I enjoyed learning about numerology science charts. It confirmed what my astrology chart revealed about my characteristics and personality but it also gave me a since of direction.

As referenced in many numerology books, charts and websites, you can discover your present career path and what you will encounter while achieving your goals. These destiny charts can be insightful and eerie. It's fascinating how these charts tell you what you will most likely experience in your life as well as what you may have experienced thus far in your life.

How you will react to a situation or a relationship is also laid out for you in your chart.

Numerology science is the study of hidden meanings of numbers and their influence on human life and believed to have been used for over thousands of years. Number values are assigned to the letters in your name.

Numerologist will then add those in a multitude of combinations with your birth date, to establish your key numbers. These key numbers are then interpreted. The numbers of your birth date reveal the path you have chosen to fulfill your mission in life and your present and future growth cycles. The numbers of your name reveal your inner feelings, personality and destiny or success of your life mission.

For those of you that are lost in your life, the information I've presented thus far is for you. For those of you that need to know a little more about the direction your life has taken, this information is for you. For those of you that don't believe in anything I've said thus far, you remind me of myself before I started reading and practicing this information.

I have been with the transportation company about two yrs when I'm approached by one of the senior drivers. He complimented my work ethics and asked me if I had ever thought about driving one of the semi trucks. I told him I was very interested and didn't know how to get started. He told me about the company training program and offered to train me on his off days. But I had to show up, rain, sun or snow because he was investing his personal time, but only if I can be dedicated.

You all, I met him every training session until I was ready to train with the company driver. He even talked the Supervisor into letting me jocky trailers around the yard and back them into the dock so I could practice my backing technique, after my shift was over. For those of you that don't know much about semi trucks, backing a fifty-three ft trailer between two fifty-three ft trailers is very challenging. Because until you master backing up, your eyes will be jumping, legs will be shaking and your nerves will be bad as hell.

About six weeks later, I was ready for testing. I took my test and passed it. All I had to do now, was wait for an opening. It was taking forever, because we had to bid for an available time slot. I was far down the bid board and it would take a year or more and that still wasn't guaranteed because you could get bumped by a driver with more seniority that wanted your time slot.

So I started putting my applications in with other national trucking companies for a full time driver and was willing to stay on with my current company

Think about how reality TV has hit an all time high. More true stories are on the rise and the truth is people, some of us are still not ready to open our minds to what is evolving around us.

We can't peel some of you away from the horror of reality, and the more gruesome the more we want to slow down and take a peek. You all know where I'm going right? We can't pass an accident on the side of the road that has smashed cars all to hell and half of us are hoping to see the condition of the people's bodies. Especially, if there is a white sheet thrown over someone. We want to see if there is a lot of blood or someone maimed.

We don't care that we've created a massive traffic jam. Some of you have the nerve to pull over, get out the car and walk up to the accident to get a close up. You will even go up to the paramedic and ask what happened. Then once you are back in your car and on the way to your destination, you will call someone else and tell them about the entire scene.

 Are we addicted to pain and suffering? It seems like the more blood that's shed the more some people want to see. These same people will hear a bump in the night and run toward it instead of away from it.

So, let me tell you a story. When I was young, we stayed in a house that I now know had a ghost. The owner died in the house and refused to move on to the after life. Y'all, I can't remember all the times I heard the toilet flushing and the water running in the sink in the bathroom across from my bedroom. My sister and brothers bedrooms were also upstairs.

I didn't think anything of it. I figured one of us got up, used the restroom and left the water on. I slept light. So, I would get up and turn the water off and go back to bed. A couple of times I woke up and my mother was standing in the bathroom with the bible open and reading scriptures.

My mother is a God fearing woman and very strong in character. I've woke up to her praying over us so much, I thought she was blessing the house from the bathroom. We stayed in that house for several years and this pattern of me getting up and cutting off the water and waking up to find my mother praying in the bathroom went on for a while so I thought nothing of it; I was too young.

Eventually, it happened less and less until I really couldn't remember when I had witnessed the last episode. Some years later, when I was an adult, we were at a family gathering.

We were talking about spirits and my mother calmly said something pertaining to the ghost that she prayed out of the house. Before she could finish what she was saying, a reel of events played back in my mind within seconds. She looked at me and I said I remember the toilet flushing and the water running in the sink. She explained that it was the person that owned the house and they died in the upstairs bathroom. They loved the house and wasn't ready to let it go yet. I'm telling you all, If my feet could have moved, I would have taken off running, just because I knew it was the truth.

I remembered feeling a presence but I didn't know what it was. My mother did mention, as I started to remember more and more, the ghost wasn't mad, they just wasn't ready to pass over. Needless to say, this is one of many reasons why I've never been a big fan of horror movies or books.

Chaos and Karma

ON my journey I found some thing continuous that is not bound by time but by circumstance. To be aware of its very existence is to be enlightened. It makes you want to watch your step.

My blessing is that I read enough about Chaos and Karma when I was young and its possible ramifications has always stayed in the back of my mind. The "what if" its true? As I've journeyed through my life, it has surfaced in my life as well as others around me. When there is no possible physical explanation why me and many others have gone through tribulations, I can say, "that's Karma."

I came across readings of the science of Karma and Chaos, written by Paul Fleischman M.D. and Forrest Fleischman. They wrote that the twelve-fold chain of causality, the relationship between cause and effect is the principle that everything has a cause according to the Buddha teachings.

The essence of this realization is predicted upon the existence of rebirth. He saw life as continuously and comprehensively lawful, a product of the ramification or consequence of action moving from life to life, across the barrier of death. Because all suffering is caused... often by deeds in the past lives and can also be eliminated when the cause is erased. Liberation from suffering or enlightenment, consists of understanding and acting upon the cause and effect relationship by which Karma leads to suffering or alleviates it.

Some students fully embrace karma as the dogma of an orthodoxy in a self-gratifying, fairytale manner, that prevents the very inquiry into causality that the Buddha intended his teaching to evoke.

Other students explained that there are moral ramifications of your behavior during life, but not before or after, since there is no before or after life.

They stated, although we have some power to change, and although our current life follows the laws of cause and effect, our birth does not follow those laws. It is an irony that this world view, which is often mislabeled scientific, is based on a serial suspension of causality; cause and effect.

The implication of chaos in comparison to karma is that, in highly complex systems like the human being, causality operates in orchestrated, comprehensible ways that reveal coherence in the phenomenal world. The chaos theory provides another way to envision a world of unbroken causality based on an open-ended sense of time and space.

These days are so crucial for all of us. The world is in chaos. Keep in mind that in the times of chaos, we must remain as calm as possible and not add energy to this storm of negativity. It surrounds all of us waiting for the moment to trip you up or catch you not paying attention. You'll know when chaos is present in your life. It shows itself in many ways.

Have you wondered about that irritable feeling that comes from nowhere? Sometimes it's so great that you become aggravated and take it out on those you love or are closest to you at the time. Open your mind and learn to control this urge that can potentially have you so removed from yourself that you leave room for someone else to start chipping away at other parts of your life.

This is no accident. Someone is always watching and waiting to take advantage of something or some part of your life that's going good. There is always going to be people that think you don't deserve what or who you have and they should have it. It's simple as that. So for you to wake up and be selfish or ungrateful any day of your life probably isn't a good thing. Just like you receive blessings, they can pass you up.

Sometimes we tend to forget where we came from. I would recommend you find yourself as soon as possible, before shit starts to happen so-to-speak. This is why chaos can find you and reap havoc on your life. The question is not if chaos will find you, but when will chaos find you?

If you're walking and living right, the passage should be quick and less irritating at the time. Remember the saying; "the devil can't come in unless you open the door and let him in." If you are not going to pay attention to what you are doing, or where you are going, then I suggest you put seven deadbolts and some chains on your front door. No! This won't keep chaos out but maybe you can feel better about what you are doing at the time.

If chaos and karma are a part of the natural energy that surrounds you, only the energy you put into the ethers will be received and returned. For those of you that think you can get a dollar out of fifteen cents, well, good luck with that.

It's like a computer program, if you program it with garbage then it will give you garbage in return and therefore you will always need an upgrade to make it better. You might as well continue to tell yourself that you are better today then you were yesterday. But, yesterday for you might be twelve to twenty-four hours ago, but for karma, it was last year when you did your wrong that now has to be made right. In short, you have to pay that bill now.

Are you ready! Will you ever be ready to pay an unexpected bill of an undetermined amount when it's time?

Think about why it's important to watch your children's path as well as your own. What if your twelve yr old shot his classmate or was the seventeen yr old that killed the police officer. The teenagers involved in the Columbine High school tragedy were absorbed by chaos. Don't forget about the innocent people caught in the path of these chaotic events.

Just when you forgot about that old bill and thought that everything is okay because you're doing better, POW! Your seed has paid that bill for you. That pain you feel from your heart being squeezed through your fingers because your seed has been taken from you, is payment in full. Ultimately, you still have to pay.

When I think in terms of the yin and the yang, negative and positive, or masculine and feminine, I also relate to chaos and karma. Take heed to karma.

We've clearly under estimate chaos and karma. Karma has a way of ensuring the right amount of payback for our wrongs so-to-speak.

You screwed up a little you have to give back a little. You screw up a lot you have to give back a lot. This could be the difference between receiving a scratch or being cut by a knife. Karma keeps the playing field fair in away. Don't take karma for granted because her wraith could mean how fast you fall from grace before being caught by that safety net.

Sometimes we become our on worst enemy. Remember, nothing or no one stays on top forever. It's inevitable. It remains to be seen how far we fall on that downward spiral. A person would use this information and build a safety net. What and how is in your capabilities but when will you start to build?

Karma is like the road that leads God's blessings right to you. But like many roads, they may have twists and turns.

So, let's say your blessing is on the road traveling in your direction and you decide to let chaos punk you into thinking it's okay to embezzle money from your company because you have a wife and a mistress to take care of, and your paycheck isn't enough to cover the expenses for two families. You probably added a curve when you started stepping outside your marriage initially.

When you decided to continue to escape into this line of bul*sh%# that you've convinced your self you could pull off, you added more curves, hills and valleys that made it impossible for your blessing to reach you in a timely manner. Now, you've pissed off karma and your blessing is on a slow boat to China. Your blessing even has time for sight seeing; after all, what's the rush?

You don't deserve it anyway! You now have to pay for what you've done and you're not in charge of the amount due. That's why everyone says, "karma is a bit*=!"

Karma is the payback queen from the havens. You always have a tab running and an account to be settled. The clock starts earlier then we think. It would be wise not to put yourself in situations that may add to your tab. You may need to remove yourself from what or who ever may upset the balance of your life and your tab.

What about your tab? Have you checked your balance lately? Do you know what has to be paid for in your future before you invite someone else into your life? No! That's the scary part. We're all stepping out on faith.

Do you have that thought from time to time about the glass being half full or half empty? Behind that thought, don't you wish you could fill the glass back up in some way to make things right again? As they say, "wouldn't that be grand in the scheme of things?"

It Continues To Evolve

I see the world as a book that I must study. I have a genuine admiration and respect for its beauty as well as its wraith. Like my life, I have slowly taken the time to feel the nuances of its differences. My journey has made me respect it. It is to be reckoned with; I have witnessed some of its breath taken beauty at various moments and places through out my life. But, I have also lived through some of its treacherous rain, snow and windstorms.

I have grown to love and fear its evolution. It's amazing to know we are connected to each other at the core. I have accepted its ability to make my body feel grounded to it's surface as I walk under the umbrella of it's sky. It was truly second nature for me to feel its currents surrounding my body as I swam in the ocean off Cancun on one of my visits.

I love swimming under water because it's calming, but it's also sensual. It's definitely another world. We have intelligent life under water that amazes me with every encounter. The water drives my love for yachts and meditation.

I've meditated through my life's shortcomings. It's helped me calm down my inner self for a moment so I can think. Sometimes, I have to many thoughts running through my mind at the same time.

I have to connect to a resource that will do what I need, when I need it, so I meditate to find peace and separate my thoughts.

All of the information I've read in those five years enlightened my mind, spirit and soul in more ways then I could have imagined. I keep experiencing a higher level of acceptance each time I allow this knowledge to guide me. If you think about it, it makes sense that our spirit enters our bodies at birth and exits after death.

However, the death and rebirth cycle is continuous throughout our lives. We can experience this cycle when we grow from the beginning to the end of one decade.

Keep in mind that the planet has a death and rebirth cycle as well. One example is the four seasons; spring, summer, winter, and fall.

Have you noticed that the weather is getting worse; that's another result of evolution. You need to stay tuned in to your surroundings. Can you see the similarities; *Revelations* and evolution, death and rebirth? Timing people...it's all about timing!

This is another wake up call for us or maybe it's a warning! The Planet is evolving and turbulent energy is roaming. Pay attention! Don't get mad at me I'm just a messenger. Some of the people reading this book may know what I'm talking about. I'm not saying anything that you haven't heard already. I'm just saying it again because I'm one of the people who believe it has to be said until we get a better understanding. Stay tuned, because I have more.

I'm at the doctor's office and I'm using a cane so it took me a minute to get myself situated. I finally sat down, looked around, saw a *BET Magazine*, picked it up and read about black entrepreneurs. The nurse called me back, I was seen by the doctor, and I left. My next visit, I sat on the same side of the room and picked up a different month of the *BET Magazine*, read it, was seen by the doctor, and I left. My next visit, I sat on the opposite side of the room because some other patients were sitting where I usually sat.

So, I sat down, looked at the magazines and selected one on geography. I flipped through a few pages before stopping at this article about how cold the weather was getting in London.   A reporter was interviewing a researcher (he didn't want to give his exact title). The reporter was quite taken by the researcher's study of the temperatures in London. The researcher showed the reporter a graph of the cold weather trending in London.

He concluded that over the next ten to fifteen years weather will be so cold in London that people won't be able to stay outside for very long. The reporter asked how long? The researcher said not long and closed his graph and didn't say anything more to the reporter. The researcher knew that the reporter would publicize his every word and that could draw to much attention to the study and possible economic panic in London.

So I ask you, is this the real reason for the space station experiments? Are they trying to find a planet with the same atmosphere as our planet for human habitation? Remember the evolution thing I mentioned above, and the death and rebirth cycle? Do you think that which we came we shall return.....hummmm? If we started from the Ice Age, could we be evolving there again?

Just Because You Don't Understand

YOU should be use to hearing about spirits and ghost by now with all the movies and TV shows dedicated to ghost chasing, tracking and various hunted encounters reported by people around the world. You don't have to go looking for phenomena, it's right here.

On my journey I have witnessed someone speaking in tongues. I taped them and went to have the language evaluated. We were told that the language sound like a form of Latin. I assure you this person has never read or studied any form of Latin languages. This person was also deemed demonically possessed. Now, this stuff took me the longest to wrap my brain around. But after a few encounters and some very real feedback from ministers, you put one and one together and come up with "what in the living hell" is going on? It will make you run around the block a few times. But, when you stop, you still have to deal with what just happened before your eyes and ears. If you are lucky, the hair on your arms and the back of your neck will have stopped standing on end and that weird presence you feel will go away soon.

But people, remember, just because you don't understand certain phenomena, does not mean its not happening to you or around you at any given time. Trust me on this. The need to understand why certain things are happening around me is what drove me to this "crazy" that I now know and understand as "awareness". I will never understand all of our natural phenomena and our unnatural phenomena, or what we refer to as our supernatural.

Come on now, you have to admit, there has been some strange shit happening around the world and the movie industry has tried to capture some of it in bits and pieces. Keep in mind that the occurrences that we are witnessing today didn't just start happening. We've been introduced to fictional and non-fictional events through movies, television and books. But a lot of our induction has come from our own experiences. Also keep in mind that a non-fictional story can have a certain amount of truth? Look at the direction so-called scary movies have taken. There are very few made-up monsters and a lot more of psychotic behavior, extreme war movies, extreme religious movies, fictional and non-fictional phenomena movies.

For those of you that remember movie's like "The Ring" and "Newborn" that showcase spirits from the after life.

What about the TV show *Medium*? It depicts a woman communicating with dead people and having the ability to read peoples thoughts.

The *Medium* is an actual person and the sitcom is based on experiences of this person. She has to except the fact that she is different. She has to deal with the phenomena that she can talk to dead people a.k.a. ghost. Some people say that this is a curse and others say it is a gift.

You will think you are crazy and other people will think you are crazy as well. But the truth of the matter is, there are many people who have this ability and are terrified to tell anyone but their religious leaders.

I think that would be my first choice if I woke up having a conversation and realized that it was indeed a dead guy.

Keep in mind that spirits are born into the flesh. This was written to help us understand the difference between ghost and spirits; "When we die some spirits move on and some stay behind. The ones that stay behind are considered ghost. Spirits cross over but can return to help us in a way. Some of us swear we were guided by a late relative or friend on occasion. It's their spirit that has come back to guide us", as reference by Shirley MacLaine. She has written movies and books revealing phenomena that she witnessed through out her life. She talked openly about her abilities to deal with ghost and spirits.

Clearly, as a human race we want to know more and more about our psyche, the supernatural, and the kinetic energy that encompasses our life. Which means I'm not the only one who has had their psyche awaken. People are waking up all around the world. That is why it's damn near erotic when I think about it.

Some of us have had premonitions, are aware of what they are and can't wait until they unfold or show their clarity. Some of us have had premonitions and don't know how they differ from our dreams.

A dream is a series of thoughts and images during sleep and a premonition is an intuition or a strong feeling that something is about to happen.

A lot of us have had premonitions but may have also confused them with de`ja` vus or even day dreams. But try to understand the differences because awareness is in the meaning.

I have experienced all of the above but not at the capacity of a so-called prophet. We are familiar with the term false prophets and recognize good prophets. For me, a good prophet interrupts a message that will come to pass.

Let me tell you about another happening that I have seen, come to pass. This was in the mid eighties, on an ordinary day, I was in the supermarket and while standing in the checkout line I saw a newspaper that had a picture of the *Prophet Nostradamus*. The heading read, "The fall of great leaders and two would be Kings". In my world at that time, I related his prediction to the following events. I remember thinking that *Nostradamus* was a myth and the tabloids are full of it anyway. But, Jim Baker and Billy Graham fell from grace and both were deemed religious leaders. I thought about the newspaper story and then I thought, no way; it was just a coincidence.

Some years later, I'm in the line at the supermarket and again the tabloids say Nostradamus also predicted two terrorist and the paper referenced that one of the terrorist would be harder to deal with.

When I first heard about Saddam and he was labeled a terrorist and was giving our government problems with the oil and everything else, it didn't come to me. But When Bin Laden join the picture, I was taken back to the moment I saw this newspaper again.

I also remember the some of the televised trial of Oliver North. He referred to Bin Laden as the most evil man he'd ever encountered and truly feared having come in contact with him. The presidency knew about Bin Laden over twenty yrs ago. So he didn't miraculously appear out of thin air or on this countries radar. Bin Laden, was grossly under estimated by our nation's leaders.

We get so rapped up in drama and placing blame that we take our eye off what's truly important. Again, we were focusing on trying to topple Oliver North instead of leaving that for the background and focusing on Bin Laden.

I will say it again; when we think in terms of priorities, don't leave something that can be taken care of today, to be taken care of tomorrow.

Did 9-11 have to happen?

I have encountered many small phenomena that have shown me every thing does have its place in the order of life. It's how we interrupt its meanings and chose to accept it or not. I thought that only a few people were born with certain gifts or abilities, but as I have found out, we all have abilities.

What about Gemstones and Herbs

ON my journey of the discovery of gemstones and chakras, I ventured into the healing theory of crystal gemstones. As I said earlier, the one I kept with me constantly is the quartz crystal because it has shown me some of its abilities to connect itself to the energy within me.

For instance, I laid it on the table and completed the steps in activating the crystal by cleaning it and blessing it with an affirmation. Yes, this is what the instructions told me to do. Then I placed it on my body and meditated.

I completed my instructions by getting up from the table and walking across the room and through the first floor of the house. The crystal freely clung itself to my chest vertically. Now, I know what you all are thinking, but my chest isn't that blessed y'all. The temperature of the crystal had gone from cold to very warm and I felt the heat against my skin.

I can feel the gemstones energy radiating from the ground through my body as it generates an antenna for clairvoyance.

While trying to find what makes me feel energized by studying quartz crystals, I found theories that the quartz crystals acts like a tool that allows not only the earths energy to past through it on to me, but solar and universal energy as well.

A natural replenishment of energy is key for me.

It could be because the earth has composite, silica and crystal embedded in its body is why I felt such a connection to the mountains. Another book suggested putting it in the sunlight for reactivation. So, I did. Plus I had a headache but couldn't lye down. I proceeded to drive to my next appointment holding this crystal on my forehead for about twenty minute's. Busy reading the directions to where I'm going, it took me a minute to realize my headache had subsided. Of course I thought it was a fluke, so I tried it again and again.

I don't know about you all, but you don't have to keep proving something good over and over again. Just like you don't have to keep acknowledging something is bad time after time.

Hey, if you find something that works, it doesn't matter if it's crystals, roots or swimming ten laps in a pool, use what ever method that helps you heal your body and mind.

But for me, one good thing lead to another and when I found out about crystals having a connection with chakras, I was hooked.

Chakras are said to be our deepest connection to our body and the earth. It is described as our instinctive urge for survival. It is the center of our being.

The seven chakras start at the top of our head and run down our spine to the tail bone. These vital areas are associated with the colors of the rainbow and when we connect to our chakras through meditation, we can rejuvenate that energy that our bodies have released through out the day and week.

I rotate between methods to not only practice the different techniques but to experience it. Focusing on my chakras awakens different parts of body as I breathe in pure thoughts. It has made me feel up lifted in nature as I start out my day or end my evening.

The quartz crystal, like many gemstones are mined from mountains, sea caves and regions that allow the temperatures to form gemstones. These stones are formed with many of the same minerals that are already present in our bodies.

So when you see the old western movies and the Indians placing gemstones over the body of someone that was ill or hurt, it was because they believed and had witnessed the healing properties of gemstones.

The Indians were also big fans of herbs for making healing teas and salves. As a matter of Indian history these teas and salves helped healed themselves and many wounded white men at a remarkable rate. It was the white man that took old Indian herbal medicine and marketed it for profit. This would also be the part of history that later moved into the era of the FDA (Food and Drug Administration). Which is one of the governments leading administrations in our country. However rumor has it...oh the hell with rumors, we all know the government regulates the FDA and if people used herbal remedies to heal themselves, the prescription drug market would have taken a nasty hit.

I continually mention timing over and over again because herbal remedies and healing books have finally been acknowledged and demanded by the consumers of our nation.

We are behind many countries in using herbal remedies. Our government was slow to approve the mass marketing and usage of herbs and we were afraid to change our thinking or do our research to validate herbal usage. After all, the government wants to control anything that affects their pockets. Herbs are used by many cultures because of the results and the affordability.

In our money hungry world, that just won't do. When it was time to check out these herbal remedies for myself, I went to the herbal store and flipped through several books although my friend, whom actually started this voyage with me, had given me the name of an author. She said that the herbal healing remedies book by *Jethro Kloss* was highly recommended from a friend of hers.

After looking at several books we found the book we were looking for and quickly flipped through some of the pages. The illnesses and remedies were from the common cold to cancer. We looked at each other in disbelief and ran to the counter to pay for the book. We hurried back to my friend's house, opened the book and slowly flipped the pages reading the names of the illnesses and remedies.

Now, don't be confused with remedies and cures. My take on remedies might be a little different then yours. I see the similarity in using a remedy 3 to 5 days and being cured rather then being told I have to take the entire bottle of pills plus a refill to be cured. That worried me. The cost difference can be huge and more important than that is the down time.

I found myself up and moving around in 24 to 48 hours and having the energy to get things done and not be contagious. In fact, as I was healing I protected myself from coming in contact with anyone that was sick so they couldn't re-infect me.

I know we all do this to some degree, with family members and ourselves that we are treating, but this was a little different. When I give medicine to my daughter I don't take the medicine to avoid being infected by her illnesses. I make an herbal remedy or tea for myself while I'm treating her so I don't get sick.

I didn't start giving her herbs until she was five yrs old and those weekly head or chest colds turned around in a few days. Now, I still took her to the doctor for respiratory illnesses and other diseases that children encounter.

But minor symptoms I treated at home and saved on a doctor's bill. If you haven't noticed the doctor's visit have long changed from "here's some medicine, take it completely and you'll be fine". You go have surgery and two to three days later you're at home self-healing with instructions.

The flu virus has changed. They don't know when you are getting over it and you can relapse from viruses two to three weeks down the road. The doctors are baffled. Just when they get a vaccine that worked, the viruses evolved. We've had some deadly viruses they believed started from mice out west and we have the viruses over seas from birds to name a couple.

We have HIV and everyone knows someone or has a loved one that have cancer from children to senior citizens. Some of the people living with AIDS have figured it out...they have nothing to loose. Some of the stories I've been told, about how herbal remedies are sustaining their lives is remarkable. People, this is no miracle kind of stuff. This is plain old lack of information.

Between the outbreak of deadly viruses and the catastrophic epidemic of Aids, people are convinced that this is the plague referenced in Revelations.

Keep in mind we are jailing athletes for supplemental steroid use while the food and produce manufactures are putting super drugs in the food to keep our population fed.

But here's the fall out once again; have you seen a twelve yr old girl or fourteen yr old boy lately! They're the height and size of a thirty yr old woman or man. Maybe its yet another secret culvert mission of the government that will back fire on the country later.

Remember we accused Russia of using steroids in their athletic programs for years. I'm just asking… "What's really going on?"

Thank God Things Change

LETS talk about how the rich is getting richer and the poor getting poorer. Have you thought about how the wealth was really suppose to be distributed. Keep in mind that there were many successful inventors who were black and never achieved the wealth to pass on to their families. To date, even though we know who the real inventors are of peanut butter, the stoplight and the carbon filament for the light bulb, etc., they have received recognition and maybe some monetary reward for their inventions, however they have never obtained the status of wealthy.

The people who had the money to build and sell these products have capitalized. They have passed their wealth onto their children and also passed on the knowledge of how to make money from other people's creations, products or services. See black people may not have had an opportunity to read, write, work or capitalize on their inventions back then. But as evolution would have it, thank God that things change!

There have been more black millionaires in the last two decades than in the history of the world, between sports and entertainment. They're buying companies, franchising in clothing, athletic apparel, liquor distribution, record distribution, food subsidiaries, car dealerships, movie theatres, restaurants, hotels, books, movies, real estate developments, etc.

Change can be a wonderful thing whether you like it or not and whether you are ready or not! So thank God for Martin Luther King and President Barack Obama.

Do you remember where you were when the reality about Christopher Columbus became a part of news channels across the nation? The Native Americans have protested for years that the information in our history books about "Christopher Columbus discovering America" needs to be changed. Christopher Columbus may have proved that the world was not flat, and that other races existed in other parts of the world, but he never truly made it to the United States of America. We now know through the history channel that the Vikings had already arrived in the Americas long before Columbus' "visited".

Who knew!

To date, that's not the only part of history that we have had to change our thinking about. What about Abraham Lincoln? He spoke about being equal to one another until his last breathe. He wanted us to think in terms of one nation. But, for me, that started the battle of the Democrats and the Republicans and it's still going on.

The Civil War was an uncivilized act against a nation, yet some of our ancestors swore the Indians and Africans were salvages and uncivilized. However, the Indians had Chiefs that kept the tribes organized, and a tribal council that helped make decisions, just as we have Mayors and council members. The Africans had Kings and council members that helped them make decisions about the tribes, just as we have Mayors and council members. The Aztecs had Kings, the Asians had Emperors, and so on.

It is a new era folks; we have to change our thinking in the 21st century. That white picket fence, 2.5 children and the happy stay at home wife is another shattered American dream that we were raised to believe, is gone.

We are a nation that resembles the story of "David and Goliath". David hit Goliath in what would be his weakest spot. After the giant fell to the ground, David was then able to destroy him. People remember, everything must evolve…nothing stays the same, and no one stays on top forever!

The attacks that happened on September 11, 2001, (9-11), was a direct hit in our weakest spot! Our pocket books!

It took the combination of 9-11 and a Republican President running our country into the ground before we would use the greatest gift that our forefathers had given us; we finally assembled as a nation for the 2008 elections.

We have spent billions of dollars just on national disasters alone, due to the increase in tornadoes, hurricanes, flooding, and hot and cold weather reaching unbearable numbers. Ice glaciers of enormous sizes are melting and moving, and a tsunami just wiped a part of the earth clean as if it were a bug on a windshield…and somewhere, someone, thought we needed a war.

The people making these decisions are your top 10% and they are led by the top 2% of the wealthiest people that actually are affected by the economic issues that the Senate and House of Representatives have to debate about. The congressional leaders have to agree whether the effects of these decisions on our economy are going to be good, bad or ugly. For those of you that don't know what I am talking about, here's a snap shot.

The Presidents are the CEOs of the business cycle, domestic and international. They allow our nation to be a financial power while controlling the GDP, GNP, and the aggregate output which is the main measure of short-term growth in our economy. After WWII the demand for consumer goods were high. But after any war consumer goods should be high because people limit their spending to primary needs and the wants can wait, as referenced in any history book!

Before 9-11 the nation enjoyed an increase in spending when the Democrats had control of the Presidency for eight years. Many jobs were created and the economy was thriving. The dollar was up in value, we had an inflated real estate market but it was booming all the same. The airline industry had competitive pricing and people could afford flying and vacationing more.

Therefore, we the people need to understand what business our country is engaged in when voting in a President to be our CEO!

I don't know about you all but I stopped spending money as soon as the Republicans took control of the Presidency. As if that wasn't concerning us enough, 9-11 dropped in and caught us with our pants off, not down, and ripped a chunk of meat right out our ass! We were definitely going to war so I stopped spending more money.

I thought we would see some of this high technology, special agent, bomb leveling stuff and these people were picking us off like a row of empty beer cans on a fence. We still haven't caught this guy!

I have to ask this question: We started a war for non-compliance of weapons of mass destruction right? While we were extending deadlines, did we not think that Saddam was smart enough to move the shit and rebuild in another area since we found out what he was doing the first time?

What's amazing is Saddam and Bin Laden knew they had time to carry out their plans because we would be tied up playing politics before we could even drop the first bomb. What in the hell is going on?

If y'all figure it out, will you call me please! I'm going to need a lot more help with this one.

Well, *Revelations* state's we will fight a holy war, a religious war. This war will appear to never end. It will change course, change clothes, and keep coming. They can't find the bad guy, because we're looking for one guy instead of realizing that we're fighting something much greater. Something we can't see, feel, or touch.

We are fighting a BELIEF!

Abraham Lincoln said it best in his speech *The Gettysburg Address*. "We should remember that the Civil War was fought and people died for their belief." Do you see where I'm going here people?

Those cultures have been fighting for many years because of their religious beliefs and what land perimeters were due to what religious sector, culture or race of people. We gave weapons to one country to fight against another country for what business deals we could make to gain allies. Which was totally illegal due to arms embargos and treaties. Our country has made some shady ass deals.

So, when they start slinging who-did-what during election time. I'm like; are you seriously kidding me! We have the *Oliver North* story. Which also mentioned Bin Laden as far back as 1987.

Now it's true, oil is the most powerful economic mineral in the world. But trust me folks, we didn't drive a *Cadillac* or a *Mercedes Benz* out of the womb and we're not driving one to our grave. It's just not that serious for some us. The leaders of our country should have invested more in alternative fuel sources way before now.

Don't be fooled by our Government, they can't protect us from this one. We wanted to be a melting pot and the stewed done burned! Thus the saying of yet another generation…"your chickens have come home to roost."   It doesn't take a scientist to figure this out. They are saying; "it's your turn", "uh huh...that's what you get", and "you should learn how to leave well enough alone".

So those of you that let the Republicans scare you into voting for them by making you think that they are not scared to fight a war to protect our way of life from the big bad wolves should now see that what they said and what really happened, was two completely different things! Now I'm not saying that our way of life wasn't effected by 9-11, I'm saying if your local police department can't protect you from a possible crime in your neighborhood or community, the army can't protect you from a possible crime in your neighborhood or community.

We have to be pro-active in our way of life and remember that things aren't the way they use to be in the 60's or 70's.

For instance, when my daughter was eight years old, she couldn't leave the cul-de-sac even if all the doors and windows were open for clear visibility.

I would sit in the doorway just so she could play or ride her bike outside. She had a better chance of staying outside longer if one of the adult neighbors was outside with their children or working in their yard. She will not experience the level of independence you want your children to achieve by a certain age, because of the types of crimes being committed against children are not just more violent, they are happening more regularly. We have to take certain precautions and police our own families and our individual way of life instead of expecting our Police departments and Army to fix everything!

All I'm saying is..."who knew"? Now we all know! So when the President asks you to help the country by being conservative with your fuel usage. We may need to adjust our attitudes and realize that if we didn't consume as much fuel we could help the price of fuel go down. Pay attention to your own life-style and be prepared to some degree for what ever may or may not happen, right in your community. This new enemy has old hate and looks like a good guy.

We don't help each other like we use to back in the day. Hell we can't! No one knows who the enemy is anymore! Is it the priest in church? Is it the child molester that moved in the neighborhood? Is it the teacher that got pregnant by the teenage boy?

Or maybe it's the mother that drowned her kids in the tub.

Don't forget about our previous President, we were mad at him because he had oral sex with a woman that worked for him. Or is it, we were mad that he had oral sex with a woman that worked for him, while he was married? The country was split on this; the men were saying " right on dog" and the women were screaming "you asshole" among the common people. Nonetheless everyone was in an uproar.

Lets be real, the Kennedy's were doing way too much with Marilyn Monroe and Prince Charles is no angel either. Did he marry Princess Diana to have children, whom would keep the royal family going? Yes! He always had Camilla on the side and everyone knew it. So, did Prince Charles have Princess Diana killed? This case has O.J. written all over it.

We'll never know what it's like to live without fear and distrust of our transportation systems. We are damned if we do and damned if we don't. We're going to have to overcome the psychological affects of terrorism. How long will that take? It can't even start until they stop bombing. So, we have a real dilemma.

Some third world countries are use to living with gunfire regularly. We are not. Even if we did bring all of our soldiers home, they can't police all of our cities and rural areas well enough to make us feel safe.

I also was a victim to this political disaster that started draining me of all the resources I needed to grow in my second career. The economy was being sucked dry of finances and with out any recovery plans on the table, big companies, little companies and self employed businesses went into survival mode. Future business was put on hold and everyone was starting to control expenses drastically. It affected my private enterprise and delayed several ventures that would have increased my financial gain over the next two yrs. Talk about a huge impact to a small business woman. I fortunately still have my job to maintain my personal finances but also filtered funds into my business to help maintain and complete current projects.

Politics is ruthless and all of us become puns when it's time for the elections. These people will play on our heartstrings until they break, to switch the presidency from Democratic to Republican. Remember what I said about the "power of belief"?

We have to stop walking around like we don't have a say in who runs our country. The Republicans regained the Presidency because they preyed on your fears. People went running to the polls thinking this government is going to protect me. The truth is here, they can't.

People, don't miss understand the role of our government. They can help protect us abroad by fighting wars. But, if a small group of terrorists, or any militant group for that matter, attack our communities or government buildings, it's up to the local authorities, the *CIA*, and the *FBI* to get involved. Remember when the war started we were all for it. Until we found out it was going to keep going-and-going.

Now, we want them to stop fighting and they can't. This should not be a news flash, it's the same cycle that has been reoccurring through out our history. That's the thing about wars, they are easy to turn on and very, very lengthy to turn off.

People say, we shouldn't impeach a president if a war is going on? So, think about this chain of events. President Clinton's Administrations was already investigating what terrorist group was responsible for the bombing of the Navy ship and the caravan in the Sudan. Bin Laden was amongst the terrorist groups being invested at this time as well.

During this time however, the Monica story was out and the Republicans kept everyone so distracted with the sex scandal, they failed to tell us that they were still looking into the seriousness of the terrorist operation that could be responsible for these attacks!

No, no, no…that wasn't as important as a sex scandal involving the President. They were so busy trying to impeach the President and kept telling us he lied about having "sexual relations with that woman." They stayed on this story because the elections were coming up. Now, stay with me on this.

They didn't say anything about us going to war over these two attacks. They were looking for a way to damage the credibility of the Democratic Party. They kept pushing the moral behavior of the Presidency and moved right to presidential candidate Jim Kerry. He wasn't strong on abortion issues and he wasn't strong on the gay marriage issue. That really got the southern Baptist going.

By this time the Monica story had lost it's power and they had to keep driving that nail of moral behavior for the Christian voters. But that's all they could say about Jim Kerry.

The Republicans get the presidency.

Now let's go back to the attacks, which were blamed on the Democrats. Did 9-11 really have to happen? They left the country unattended while they played politics. The Republicans quickly stated "they, meaning the Democrats, should have taken care of this problem when they were in office." People did you read what I'm telling you thus far about the government. If you have read some of the publications from 1987 until 2001, they knew about Bin Laden. We just didn't know about Bin Laden. We didn't know they had been warned and had dealt with him way before 9-11 happened. President Clinton wanted to take military action, but no one wanted to listen to him because the Monica sex scandal had taken priority.

I have to apologize now for the things that are about to come out of my mouth about Monica.

Why did she keep the dress? I came up with two very strong reasons:

1. She needed evidence because she was going to black mail him for money to continue supporting her after he stopped seeing her.

2. She needed evidence to stay alive in case she became a liability. I have heard some very interesting comments from women with all types of status. They all seem to have a clear view on one thing; Monica didn't know how to play the game.

The white women were saying, "she should have known better!" The black women were saying, "She should have kept her mouth shut!" The Hispanic women were saying, "you stupid —BeeeeeeeeeP!"

Her life went from a nobody, to a somebody that no one liked, then back to a nobody. But, she's alive! She's banned and being treated as a leper sometimes, but, she's alive. Because that, "she did the right thing" story is not working, she's a grown woman, she knows right from wrong!

Go Fix Our Shit

IN this chapter you will find some humor and sorrow as I tell the stories of many different people and their down to earth thoughts about their lives.

Now let me tell you about another woman. She was not famous or popular, she was just an every day taxpaying citizen. She met this guy and they started dating, which led to them moving in together. Well one day out of the blue she calls her brother's cell phone as he was on his way home from work. Now, he's doing ten to fifteen years in prison because he beat her boyfriend every which way, but to death.

Why...because his sister's boyfriend had beaten her every which way, but to death. Her brother had a wife and a son at home. He couldn't believe that someone would do his sister so wrong. He couldn't help himself. He believed that his sister was a good person and she didn't deserve the beating this man put on her. He knew he was wrong for what he did, but he was so overwhelmed by the pain and suffering he saw his sister going through, he just couldn't sit there and do nothing.

The meanings behind the words, "an eye for eye" and "if you steal from me, your hand should be cut off", are very powerful, still to this day. People are willing to die for what they believe in, they are also willing to go to jail for that same belief. This man was raised to believe that a man should never lower himself by beating a woman because he couldn't control himself.

I've heard story after story. You probably have heard a story like this one. A forty-five year old man, just your every day tax paying citizen, who will tell anyone that will listen to him, that he hate's his job and have three kids and a woman at home, he doesn't like or love. So he goes home, gets drunk, yell at the kids and beat the woman down, because she won't leave. What he doesn't tell is, when she tries to leave he beats her to make her stay. What is wrong with this way of thinking? There are crazy people and there are people playing crazy, living right next door to you. Some of us really need to go fix our shit! Stop blaming every one for your personal failures.

Now, defending yourself is in the *Bible*. I don't believe in violence but I do believe everyone has a right to defend himself or herself.

For instance, If a woman name Big Bertha got you in a headlock, you might need to knock the hell out of her so you can get away. Lets keep it real y'all, there are crazy men but there are also crazy as hell women that will fight you, cut you, and shoot you, cause they don't know how to fix their shit.

I once heard a woman yelling…" he's trying to leave me for another bit#%, but not if I kill him first!" Oh yeah, that's clear right there "sista." A blind man can see that you need to go fix your shit!

Sometimes we get things turned around. This may be because of the way we were raised, or the things we were exposed to in our environment such as our homes, schools and neighborhoods.

Although our ancestors did the best they could under the circumstances in their time, we need to do better because we can. It's not written anywhere that we cannot change the way we do things just because our ancestors did it that way.

In fact pick up 1, 2, or even 5 books, out of the hundreds of self-help books out on the market that talk about nothing but helping yourself. Actually that is what this book is telling you! Some of you need to get up right now and go fix your shit! I know we can all agree that what worked back in the day doesn't work now. Stop being afraid to make the necessary changes in your life to better yourself, your children, and your situation.

Can someone tell me, why we have families on welfare for ten generations? Yes...I said ten generations. We have to agree on all levels that this is not a goal for our future. This is a double edge sword. I've seen families use social services for help when they needed help, especially if there were children in the house.

I have heard people preaching to the up coming generations about this downward spiral into the black hole of self-defeat. In my opinion no one wakes up and decides to be on welfare forever. But in a sense this is what's truly happened in some of our families.

If you think forward into the next ten years for just half of a generation of children that were raised on welfare, you see a stamp on their character and personality that reads "product of my environment". That stamp is being broadcasted to us from the inside out. They walk defeated; they stand defeated and they are truly mad as hell at the world they live in. Poor behavior is learned just like good behavior is learned.

This comes from generations of parents, grandparents and great grandparents that saw life as just getting by with a roof over their head and food in their children's mouth. They were struggling with basic survival so they only knew to teach basic survival. There are crossroads that each generation has to step on to so the bar can be raised to the next level. But, who is leading this cheer and who is supporting this forward movement under each roof.

We are quick to ridicule and slow to react to something new and positive. Some people have told me they were jealousy, some were envy and most of the people I spoke to about this subject said It's from lack of structure in the household.

We did not collectively as a household understand the future challenges that our children would face if we didn't instill certain behavior in them. The people that had a clue about what to teach their children were labeled, uppity, because they were trying to show their children how to better themselves. What they truly instilled in these children is the future that we will depend on them to take forward. The picture here has always been bigger then some people could see. We still have work to do.

If you can imagine a family of four children and each of these children had three children and each of them had two children and so on for ten generations. That is over thirty-six people with minimal education, work ethics, lacks responsibility and sociable behavior.

This translates into many things. They will struggle with keeping a job and maintaining a home. They will shy away from the benefits of being in a positive social circle. Their lack of responsibility and failure to maintain a job will frustrate them and a life of poverty and/ or crime to feed the need to eat will become a first option instead of a last option.

Many times people revert to what they know. Such as, If I get with a girl or guy and have a couple of kids I can get on welfare. The survival skills they've been taught became their immediate default.

Four to five years after High School, when they're reuniting with their peers and everyone is exchanging information about their career status is when they realize, their surviving. They are content with this thought at twenty-three years old. They don't see that huge picture hanging from the sky that shows them they are needed to hold a place. To help run communities, businesses and political offices in the future of their country.

By them over coming their challenges to achieve these goals, their children will naturally think this is the basic survival skill. It is true that our children start out as a product of us. But as they grow into an adult, I would hope they can adapt to what works in their life and throw the none working shit out!

What about the teenage mother and gang member father I met, that doesn't know enough about life to grow past their environment. They have a chance to turn that corner for the better. But all they see is gang infested territory surrounding them so they have to learn how to survive in that environment.

He became a gang member to exist in a world that he believed had status. He felt that he was raised around gangs and he turned out all right.

He and his girl friend have a two yr old son who is wearing a colored bandana and a gold chain around his neck. The mother is six months pregnant and has no goals for furthering her education or getting a job. She can get a bigger place after she has the second baby because her benefits go up. The father is working on his hustle for the day.

He did try to get a job. However, he couldn't get the job he wanted because he did time for armed robbery and the company won't hire felons. Therefore society has to put up with him continuing to rob people or homes in the community. He didn't take advantage of the free college knowledge he could have received in jail.

What he doesn't realize is that he's contributing to the high cost of car insurance and home insurance rates we pay to live in the community his stealing from. So, if their friends or family is staying or working in that community, they are stealing from them indirectly.

His first son is six years old now and he realized that he has nothing to show him but how to be in a gang. Now he wants to get a job. He still can't get the job he wants so he finally settled for working at a car wash. He could have gone back to school or went through a certified program to help get a better job. But with no one around to encourage him, he didn't see the value in more education. How it could have offset some of the hardship of his felony when looking for a job.

His girl friend saw him trying to do better and she thought this would be a good time for her to try and do something more with her life. She struggled at first because she didn't want to lose her benefits and if she couldn't make enough money to pay for daycare and pay her bills, why work?

She hasn't said anything that I haven't heard from several young mothers on welfare. Again, she's a product of a family unit that has done just enough to survive.

Well, no one would hire her. So she finally went to a temporary agency. They tested her and then gave her a suggestion. She was told that a mother with two children should go to school at her age. She could still receive some support and daycare assistances to help with her children if she's enrolled in school.

Just by trying to better your self, people will extend a helping hand. You never know what your life has planned for you but it clearly starts with your will to do better.

She uses the advice and went to college. At the end of her first year she needed to study for her final exams. She asked her boy friend to watch the kids while she did her homework. He said no and told her to get a baby sitter if she needed someone to watch the kids while she studied. She said, "you're their father and you're sitting here doing nothing, why should I pay for a baby sitter". He said, "you're the one that decided to go to school; so you can figure it out".

Frustrated, she called her mother and had her watch the kids.

The boy friend was still working at the car wash. He was upset that things had changed in the relationship. He can't work the job he wanted to work and he doesn't care to help his girlfriend in her time of need. The defeated mentally surfaced. The future of his girlfriend was second to his.

This is where behavior rears its ugly head. If you can't experience good behavior in your life then you will not have good behavior, unless you train your self to over come these challenges.

Where he should step up in his role as a father and boy friend to support her endeavors, he let his personal failure's get the best of him and put a bad taste in his girl friends mouth.

She is now pissed off and thinking about all the time she stood by him when he had nothing. What about all the time she spent making sure he had a meal when he came home. The house was clean and their children were clean. She stood by him knowing that he put her and their children in danger by being in a gang. But she stayed by his side, proving her love for him.

Him not wanting to watch his kids while she studied was like a slap in the face. She cried because she doesn't understand why he has turned his back on her. She doesn't know his heart is filled with envy.

I said, although he stopped being in a gang for a good reason, he still needs to fix his shit. He still has to change his thinking. He doesn't like this, "real life shit" as he called it and still wants to be a rebel in his heart and mind. He still hasn't moved passed the adrenaline of his superficial praises from being a well known gang member. He had a title and was recognized for who he was! So what he did time.

Being a feared bad guy can be four times as powerful then being a feared good guy.

I told her to keep in mine that he didn't have any body looking out for him and therefore he may feel he doesn't have to look out for any body!

That is the history of his behavior. Now he's at a crossroad in his life and don't even know it. He has an opportunity to pray it forward. But he doesn't know how. He has an option to call someone else and ask them what he should do but he only knows more gangs members. He can't call them because he would look soft in front of his friends. Talking to a pastor is definitely out!

So his behavior continues. He hasn't swallowed enough to get passed his pride and maybe change the way he thinks in terms of their lives together. He is stuck in a way that many young adults fall victim to; the way they were raised by their family and community.

I thought to my self he will stay in this mind set until he learns to elevate his thinking. Maybe she can pull him in to her changed thinking.

She wiped the tears from her face and looked at him, looking at TV. She nods her head one time in his direction and walked a way. Determined she would finish school, she continued to do what ever it took to raise her children. She even continued to take care of her boy friend.

Two years later, after coming home from class one day, she sat down next to him on the couch and suggested he should go to school then maybe he can get a job like the one he wanted. He gave her a few good excused as to why he's not going to go back to school then told her that just because she's going to school doesn't mean "she's better then him". She looked at him in his car wash shirt and said, " I am only better then who I use to be"!

Don't forget by bettering yourself, you could make better decisions about your life? Not just your every day life, but your entire life. If you are not successful at being you, then how can you be sure that the advice of others is good for you or not! How do you know what's not good for you? Like that man or that woman you may want to bring into your life or your children's life. Stop listening to everybody just because it's easier and make a good decision based on your own situation.

What about your own goals; you can't have goals without knowing who you are first. Nobody knows you well enough to tell you the right answer. They're merely making suggestions or sharing their opinions. But some of us are so scared to admit that we made a bad decision about our own shit. We'd rather say that I trusted my friends or another family member, or better yet; I made this very important decision about my life, because my Pastor told me to!

Now, let's not be confused about our leaders and their roles in your lives. Because, we want to rely on our pastor's to guide us through everything. We all think, "He's a man or she's a woman of God, what they say must be the truth!"

Leaders are just that. But if we don't understand the role of our leaders or our purpose for asking them for help then everyone's time is being wasted. Our leaders have to have something to work with in order to help you achieve your objective.

I think we go to them broken and want them to tell us why we're broken and how to fix it. Some of us want that all in the same sitting. Leaders can be mentors with information to share from years of experience and knowledge passed onto them from other leaders.

They can also be the messengers. Just like there are good and bad leaders there are good and bad messengers.

I kept walking and watching the leaders that I either worked with, socialized with through community services, politics or other organizations. I was a person that was always in the front paying attention to how things got done and objectives were accomplished. As I worked through my own shit, I worked my way up through corporate America, I evaluated companies and people just as they did me.

At review time I always had questions about the development plans of the company. I was trying to get a lead on where I should focus my development skills so I could become a qualifying candidate by the time the changes were implemented. I learned a lot by taking the initiative to join in conversations with peer groups higher then my own. I wanted knowledge.

Your peers on average have the same knowledge you do more on less.

If you're trying to excel in your career, it's important that you start with information that's going to take you to the level. And for those of you that have the drive to achieve more than one thing at a time, you have excelled over and over again.

Some of the young men and women from the eighties and nineties generation are already living the life of working full time and going to school at least part time just to have a chance for a descent job. What is descent? I guarantee you that it's know where close to what it was between the seventies and nineties. They will be in line with more educated people and making less money then a person with the same credentials.

For the future of our country it will be beneficial. Not just the fact that a person with a master's degree will be making $13 to $14 dollars an hour, but their will be more educated people in the work place and running the country.

Some of you all may not know this, but that is exactly why our jobs are going oversees. They don't have the robust economy that we have so everyone spends their time in school getting a higher education. Therefore, American jobs are going to India because their paying a worker $12 to $13 dollars an hour and they have a master degree. They are also living in a house in what we classify as the suburbs and have two cars. They are now living the white picket fence elusion.

Things must change. We are victims of our standards of life and I'm okay with that; but when I look back at the leaders of our country, I do have questions. Such as: where did the preventive measures go? I remember when I was able to go to the community center and play with my friends after school. Be a part of a community project or basketball team. We learned how to be a part of many team sports and activities. Being a part of the community center helped everyone with their social skills.

I remember when the funding was cut for the community centers across the country but particularly in our neighborhood. That is when the hanging out on the corner began. We had a bunch of displaced kids that was use to going to after school activities, to doing nothing. For some, they lost the only mentor they had in their life at that time. A lot of teenagers hung out on the corner because they had no place to go. They would meet up like they were going to the center and fifteen to twenty teenagers would be hanging around on the corners by the center.

One corner was as good as the other so they started hanging on any corner.   This increased the gang activity and the drug dealing activity for many neighborhoods in our communities. Everyone became more aware of the increased bad guys in the neighbor and started locking every door and window in their homes and cars. Petty break in crimes were on the rise and everyone wanted to fight. Some weeks it seemed like we fought our way home every other day after school. Teenagers were just angry about change and didn't know what to do with them self.

Some of us got reeled in by our parents and read the riot act about graduating with out a police record. My mother wasn't having that nonsense and drama at her house with her children. She talked to us constantly about being aware of our actions, where we were and what we were doing in between school, other   activities and home.

She let us go to activities where our schoolmate's also attended but we had to go home afterward. We couldn't hang around in the streets and possibly in up in juvenile detention. Oh no; we didn't have that kind of mother. My mother demanded respect from us and that's what she got. If fact, as I've mentioned, we had strong women in our family and they all demanded respect.

We were taught that your actions now could limit your opportunity in the future and that was a very real conversation in our house.

I know we've talked about the generations from the late eighties and nineties and their disrespectful behavior toward their elder's and peers. They don't care about respecting others but want to be respected and don't really know what that means.

It's not relative to gang respect but gang respect wants to be relative to the true meaning of being respected. Respect as referred to by the thesaurus means: A deep admiration for someone or something elicited by their abilities, qualities and achievements.

Thus the saying that respect has to be EARNED! But it also has to be taught and recognized. Unlike the respect gang members acquire from instilling fear, to respect the quality of a persons character and admire their achievements, they are worthy of true respect.

In the mid to late seventies, the reported cases of child abuse were off the charts. This increased social services awareness in the schools and empowered teachers to report suspected abuse of children. That was a great idea and it clearly identified the children that were from abused homes.

The message was taken advantage of by other children. The message basically told children if they were being abused/hit at home they could come to school and report it and they would be put in a place where they wouldn't be abused.

Now we all know there is a difference between discipline and abuse. However, something in the message "report abuse to a teacher at school" gave some children the ammunition to use against their parents.

Children of all ages started getting away with disrespecting their parents as well as their teachers and any adult. They went from being contained to being undisciplined and totally out of control. They became hard to live with and aggressive. They were threatening their parents that if they talked to them a certain way, they would go to school and tell their teacher that the parents were abusive.

We were talking about it at work as if it were the topic in a magazine. We couldn't believe the advantage pre-teens and teenagers were taken of their parents. Parents were being threatened because they told their teens to do home work or chores. It was so bad that parents had to give their teens the option of staying at home and doing what they were asked to do or leave. Parents were put on the defense as if trying to be a good parent wasn't hard enough.

If your child screamed abuse, you have to go to court, you may get charged with child neglect and lose a day of pay over a very true statement, you're about to tell the Judge; "Yes, your Honor I was going to put my child on a punishment because they didn't do their home work and when they disrespected me by yelling and telling me what they weren't going to do, I was either going to knock the hell out of them or put them out my house".

In the twentieth century we have more parents killing their children for various reasons, taking guns to work and shooting co-workers. Teenagers are killing their parents and other adults, shooting up high schools and killing other children. This is happening more than ever before in the history of our country. We can clearly see that it's from dysfunctional families as well as so called normal families. From foster parents and foster children to grandparents and grandchildren, the chaotic energy is swallowing people up.

The frequency of these horrific events has shocked us all and left us wondering when is this craziness going to end? Just when we think one incident is the worst we've ever heard on the news, another one happens and leaves us speechless. This is some shit that still has to get fixed.

I believe, the direction of someone's life can be according to the road map of their destiny if they chose to find tune their insight. With out faith, fear will consume us and our decisions will be based on confusion.

I have to reference Confucius, an ancient Chinese thinker and Philosopher. His teachings emphasized personal and governmental morality, correctness of social relationships, justice and sincerity among the Chinese, Korean, Japanese and Vietnamese. Confucius thoughts have been developed into a system of philosophy compiled into a collection of "brief aphoristic fragments" after his death. His great quotes are apart of a scientific principle such as "if it ain't broke, don't fix it".

So when I think of the senseless killing from the hands of parents on their children and from children on their parents, one of Confucius quotes come to mind; It said "We should feel sorrow, but not sink under its oppression". The mind has to be in a state of persecution for a person to carry out these actions.

It's hard for people to believe the demons embedded in their soul and how quickly they surface.

I know that my spirit is strong but my flesh is weak. I know that my mind is powerful and has to be controlled as much as possible. Because if you make up your mind that you are going to kill today. Then you will kill. The mind is not to be under estimated. It will over rule the heart and spirit and proceed forward with whatever detriment its going to cause.

After talking to many inmates from strangers to family and friends. They have all expressed how strong their thoughts become when they're angry. Some of them have referenced the smell of blood when they're angry.

Could this be why some of our black men are in prison. It's hard for them to acknowledge that mechanism with in them that say's... stop! They would have to be open to the second part of their nature and allow the heart and spirit to join forces in order to change their mind. Don't wait until the aftermath clears to realize you should have hit the stop button. Especially when you know you're doing something wrong.

This is a part of behavior easily accepted from one man to another, father to son or mentor to man. But is takes a man to tell another man of any age about controlling the beast within. Maybe this is why it appears that our black men are still incarcerated in their mind. Again, behavior has to be taught and learned. If there is no one to teach them, they can truly become lost and taken advantage of by your mind.

Black women have told me time and time again how they need their men back from the penial system. I can feel this truth because although an incarcerated man can receive education in prison, he cannot learn the bonding to a family while he is kept from a family. We cannot substitute the bonding of children and companion or sister and brother or mother and father. It must be lived and learned. This is that same bond that has been broken for over two hundred years of slavery.

I say again, Black women want their black men back and this is some shit we still have to fix.

From young to old, we still don't have enough of our black men trying to over come their social challenges. For the most part, it's because they don't know how. But the majority, don't seek out the information to help with this transformation. Some of them are fighting hard not to acknowledge their second nature. As referenced by science, men and women have each other's nature. Some of our black men fight this part of them self full time.

But in doing so, could it be they are blocking that mechanism they tells them to stop! For some reason they believe by acknowledging their second nature, their going to wake up soft hearted or worst, GAY! For some reason they equate this acknowledgement with being a punk. They have totally over looked the fact that they need this part of them to expand their thought process.

There second nature is the part that talks them out of doing stupid shit. You know, like a girlfriend or wife would. This is the part that allows them to have continued growth, mentally and emotionally. That growth is a part of their life cycle and they limit their social skills and other economic skills when they don't acknowledge their second nature.

Growth has to struggle instead of blossom.

When talking to men in their thirties, they understand what they should have done to finish raising them self, but has lost a lot of time. They believe there's no reason to better them self at this point. Until they meet that woman. She has brought out the best in him and he doesn't know where to get the best of him. What they said was, they don't know how much they need to better them self to get her stamp of approval. If the effort becomes more then they are willing to give, then the all stop button is pushed.

They can't reason why they should put them self through all this trouble for a woman who will leave me for another guy anyway. The "anyway," means; they know they should have taken the time to start bettering them self before now. The truth is, we still don't have enough black men taking the initiative to better them self just for them self or teaching this behavior to younger black men. They need to be ready for their life and that relationship. Instead they wait. Then when they feel the pressure from a woman telling them to take the time to better them self, she's being unreasonable.

So I asked; have you realized your expectation of her? You want her to be understanding and wait for you to grow into this person that was lacking social skills. You were in prison so she has to deal with you over coming that mental status that also affects your ability to grow.

Just because she agreed to stand by your side, you think that she's not watching you so you slow down your development pace. However, she continues to grow. Two years with someone is a long time. It's longer when you're expected to see increased growth. She's at her deadline to see results from you and now she's ready to move on with out you.

A few of them replied; F%#K her then!

Excuse me! Why are you mad at her? You have no one to be mad at but your self. You have minimized the expectations of your self. Her expectations of you are to do what you say you're going to do.

Black women want to support their black man that is head of their household. He has gained their respect, trust and confidence. They see him working his mind and body for the benefit of the family. They will respect him for being a provider and they will learn from his strength.

His son's will have control of their inner beast because his children will depend on him to teach them how. They will learn to support their family as he support them until they reach that age when they can teach and support them self.

His daughter's will look for this pillar of strength in the man she selects to be her head of household. She will admire his soul that he bares for his family and his self. She will brace him up when he is leaning and let him lye his head in her bosom when he is tired. She will be his right hand, his partner, sister and mother when she needs to support his mind. They will become each other's true opposites and together they will covet their nest. Their bond has to be the strength of steel. The respect for each other's character can only grow in a healthy and vigorous way. They will learn to move pass their petty differences and become victorious over their adversaries in order to reach this common goal of raising a family.

I feel we must let go of our egos and be centered to let our true inner person of strength reveal itself. There is a place and time for the beast within us all to surface and defend or protect us from danger. However, don't let your inner beast be the determining factor on how you want to live your life. Why not wake up and feel the heat from the sun on your body. Why not be able to look up at the blue sky and go anywhere you want whenever you want.

As long as God allows you to wake up, the world is your playground. Don't justify confinement to your self. It's not okay. You are excepting confinement as something that can be achieved. Did you miss the history lesson my strong black brothers and sisters? Our ancestors survived confinement at the highest level...death. Their lessons teach us that we can endure anything. They paid the price so our race can continue to exist on the strength within us all.

I know it's hard for some black women and men to grasp that very part of their history that could tell them who they truly are and who their ancestors were.

So when we voluntarily sign up for confinement, by not being able to control our inner beast, it could indeed be a slap in the face of our ancestors. There is no need to confine our minds, bodies or souls. The choice to be free and remain free is very challenging and we have to reach deep within our very core to forgive that wrong doer in order to remain free. To not forgive only defeats...you.

Past to Present

IT will be important for me not to shake or quiver on my journey because there is always a negative energy lurking near by to impede your success. Negative energy or people are like opportunist. They lay and wait for the time to encourage fear and failure. You will be left confused and disoriented as it swarms around you.

That is where the saints come to my rescue, particularly, John the Conqueror and Saint Christopher. I call on them to help me conqueror my fears of trying and to help guide me on my way.

I can't help thinking how some of us barely know whom our living relatives or our ancestors are. What about what they stood for and died for. How could we miss the relative pattern of strength that our culture represents? We need to share with our children the success and failures of their ancestors. It is important to know who else was successful amongst their relatives.

Remember the statement, "together we stand and divided we fall." Some of us need to keep practicing on the standing part. We need to strengthen that family structure like a knot. Life is way to short and we all know it. I'm trying to enjoy everyday God let's me wake up. I'm going to spend as much time with as much of my family and my daughter as I possibly can. I will not let myself be misled by false prophets or poor leadership. I will steer my ship on a steady course on my destined path.

I think about the stories I have heard about my ancestors and how determined they were to move north. Their journey took them to Gary, Indiana before settling in Benton Harbor, Michigan. One story in particular that comes to mind is about the car they drove for the trip. The car was so beat up mechanically that they had to stop after so many miles and fix it when it broke down...thank God they were mechanically inclined. Well, they knew that the car could possibly break down along the way so that was the determining factor on who would be the ones to go on that trip.

They also needed room for the gas that they traveled with. Yes... they had the gasoline in the car with them, and food too. Therefore when they stopped they fixed the car, gassed up, and ate all at once. They never got off to the road they were travelling. My heart beats differently every time my mother tells a family member about their troubled filled journey. I can close my eyes and imagine the determination in their heart and the struggles they had to over come in order to leave Helena, Arkansas.

What amazed me when my cousin told me this story about our ancestors is that their blood flows through my veins. Knowing that my relatives were strong and determined people have made me stand very tall. I always had big shoes to fill when I spent time with my family members. There was always someone I could look up to that represented strength in every letter of the word.

My great-great grandmother Gertrude Haire had three brothers. They were my uncles Isaiah, Jeff and York. My uncle Isaiah had twenty-one kids; you heard me right, twenty-one! I'm grateful for him because he put our bloodline on the map for a very long time. Great-great grandmother Gertrude married Mr. Tom Penson, and they had two daughters, my great grandmother Lula and my aunt Anna. My great grandmother Lula is my grandmother Julia's mother and grandmother Julia had a daughter, Janel, who is my mother.

There was my aunt Anna and her daughter's Rita, Ilene and Connie. My aunt Anna is stamped across my heart. She and her daughter's were very supportive of my working mother and they watched us for her from time to time. My uncle Jimmy and his daughter Magnolia whom tried to teach me how to play the piano but I sucked at it so she taught me how to swim instead.

There was my uncle Clifton Timberlake, who stood about 6'3" and weighed about 210lbs. He was a broad man and had the heart of a locomotive. He worked with his hands and got up with a purpose to fulfill and that's what he did. Whenever I think about the stature of some of our male ancestors, I think about the broad shoulders and hard working man that my uncle Timberlake.

We also grew up with my father's side of the family. My paternal grandmother was Ninnie B, and she had two sons, my father, Hosea Oliver, and his brother Andrew. My uncle Andrew and his wife Bernice had seven kids. The three kids in my family and my seven cousins all looked out for each other so you couldn't mess with any one in our family without having to face all ten of us, big and small.

Our family reunions were like most reunions. They're all about keeping up with all the new arrivals to the family from babies being born to who just got married. I loved going to the family reunions so I could eat some of every thing in sight. Our relatives on my mother and father side of the family were some very good cooks. When it was time to eat at any family function I was always the first to sit down, and the last one to leave.

My mother would always look at me and shake her head in disbelief because I would eat enough food for two people. Y'all I couldn't help myself. When the food taste good you're going to eat twice as much. My mother is a very good cook and many of my friends can attest to that. No matter what part the country I lived in my mother would visit and cook up great meals.

Of course when my friends stopped by to pay their respects they all made sure it was around dinner time. Once a friend experienced my mother's cooking they always wanted more. They would ask me to bring them food back from the visits to my mother's home in Michigan. Although I eat smaller portions now, I still love my mother's good tasting food.

As we started tracing our family tree's, I've often wondered, could the same blood that runs through my veins be that of a tribal warrior?

The same brave soldiers that protected their land as well as their villages in Africa from rogue militia and terrorist. These same soldiers that fought other tribal armies over land and other political agendas, could be my ancestors.

As referenced in many books and websites, some African tribes are farmers, shepherds, Ivory and arts sellers, they were some tribes that also sold slaves. However, I am just referring to the bloodline of the tribal warriors. But when I think about the heart and soul of some my relatives and their warrior like behavior, it's like looking in the mirror and seeing the reflection of African warriors.

I dated a guy from Ghana when I was in college and he would share stories about Africa with me.   How an experienced fighter is taught the skills of fighting at ages as earliest as eight years old. He is born with the soul of a warrior and therefore his mind, body and spirit is that of a warrior. The heart of a warrior can rage like a lion ready to attack. The lion will not be confined, so he will fight. The lion will not be controlled, so he will fight.

To me the soul of the warrior and the heart of the lion are within some black men. They don't understand being controlled by others and controlling them self utilizes the same thought process. You have to control yourself in order to let someone have the power to influence or guide you. Ultimately, you are still the controller of you.

I feel that some black leaders don't express this in a way that our black men, women and youth can grasp the concept. This is an important concept to promote within the black leadership role. As leaders we are still needed to help develop the next group of leaders in our communities and families. We have to help them define, analyze, implement and monitor their small successes so they can reap the benefits of their large accomplishments.

We have to encourage families to talk about more business strategies at home and with their children. We need to teach our children about financing and investing in land and real estate. We don't have to just buy property. If we can't qualify for that house we want right now, buy a lot or two. Make sure they know what a fixed asset is and the tax credit advantages. Teach them how to manage their life style while they are still teenagers and young adults. We all have something to gain from learning for ourselves first, then passing that knowledge on to our children.

That's because your family can be a huge network of information and contacts. Now, if you're one of those relatives that have given up on life and half ass treat yourself right and don't have any self-respect, go fix yourself first. Successful relatives are people too and will not help you just because you're a relative. You are still a relative with a broken track record and may not know the difference between receiving help and wanting a hand out.

You still have to present yourself to a relative like you would any other person in your social arena. You still have to give them your resume so they can give you the necessary feed back and/or contact information.

Don't think just giving your relatives your resume is going to explain your future goals or plans either. This is an interview and an opportunity to possibly gain their support in your future endeavors.

We missed the opportunities to pool the family members together that wanted to be potential investors by creating a company each person could contribute and benefit from its growth. If ten family members put $10,000 in a business bank account, a company would have been formed with a $100,000.00 investment. That could be used for collateral and a bank loan could be borrowed against a percentage of that amount. Other family members could have been trained as employees.

This is the information that we need to pass on to our children. How to be your own boss and create a successful business. The resources to invest in a business, is right there in your family.

To me, family is important. My life weaves through theirs as I collect the hugs and support I need to replenish my hope. They become that push you need to get out of bed in the morning and that burst of energy to work a few more hours. They have watched me become the woman I am today as my Journey has taken me to away places but has returned me to them time and time again.

I awake and sleep by candlelight so it can purify my atmosphere and give my home peace. As it burns, my thoughts have clarity and some times my answers come to me in my dreams as if I was awake. In a way, the flame lights my path so I can see the breadcrumbs to follow in my mind to navigate my way on this journey through life.

It's Damn Near Erotic When I Think About It

THAT'S why it's damn near erotic, when I think about it. I visited a plateau...no! I've been to a place. It made me feel not on this earth. I felt light and weightless. I unknowingly had an experience and I've spent the last ten years of my life trying to deny it happened. I was scared to share it with anyone because I was afraid they would call me crazy. Guess what? I've been called crazy because I work too much. Don't be afraid to be called crazy, it may help keep the other crazy people away from you.

Maybe it was the fear of not wanting to let go of that last little piece of lust, the bad, and the ugly of my life, as I know it. See, when I was writing this book I thought to myself, people are going to question who I am because I have a mixture of reality, science, phenomena and religion in the same book and even on the same pages. The religious people won't like that and I may not sale enough copies of this book. The scientists has to have a reason that everything happened and they will discredit the phenomena in the book. There are many different people in this room and in every arena no matter what the event, they will not like this book.

Finally, I stopped second guessing myself. I wanted to tell you about my journey. I realized when I was writing this book, it wasn't just for you all, it for me. It's a part of accepting who I am, where I've been and where I'm going. I had to grow into who I am, just like you have to grow into who you are. It is your destiny as it is mine. It is the power of acceptance! I can't live for you I can only live for me. You do not have to like me because I am different, but if I have shown you no disrespect, all I ask is that you show me no disrespect. If I have not caused you any pain, I ask that you not cause me any pain.

You see, at some point in our lives we have to get it. We have to understand why it was written that Jesus Christ died for our sins. He did not die because everyone in the world was good. I now know that it was because we were different. We were not born with eternal beauty. I feel that he knew it was going to take us time to grow into the understanding of what that means.

Just like I wrote this book to appeal to a broad audience. He knew that it would take us time to grow into the understanding of who we are and what we are apart of. You must speak in many different languages to get a message to a broad audience. You must be prepared to stand tall while you're being ridiculed.

I do not apologize for delivering the message, only for some of the offensive language that was used to creatively capture my audience, who other wise might not have listened to the message. In my lifetime, I've seen the communication railroad go through many changes for the young, middle aged and older audiences.

Marketing a product can take some strange appearances and under tones. And can you believe the language they used! My answer at my current age is yes. But more then that, did the message penetrate a higher percent of listeners? That is what has to be measure today. Because if the message didn't reach a variety of listeners, the fallout or adaptation to the message will not be seen for years. We've closed the gap with the Internet and the media.

But have you noticed how creative, blunt, and down right nasty some of the visual effects and the language has become. Take video games for instance. We market a product for immediate sales by effectively targeting a certain group or generation. Visual effects capture your attention by causing some kind of blunt force trauma to your memory. We have realized this works and now you see dramatic types of marketing the include visual or special effects for products of all ages. The world took its next step into the future by way of space age and technological advancement. We have arrived so-to-speak.

Now, where do you fit in all of this? Where are you going? Will your same daily routine fit inside this global change? Have you thought about your next five years of living? Most of us are still in the "we will have gas forever" cloud. Have you been paying attention?

The country is under terrorist attack from it's own citizens as well as foreigners from other countries and the world is being visited by beings from other planets. Yes, I said it again, other planets! A well-known scientist recently said on TV "if we inhabit this planet, it is ridiculous to think that other planets are not inhabited by some form of life." People open your minds, look in the newspapers from 1942 to 1952 and thru President Jimmy Carter's administration. In fact, read some of the chronicles about visitors from other planets that have been published against the recommendation of the Presidents of our country.

While living in Denver, one of my jobs was a supervisor of security for Stapleton Airport. This particular day I was covering one of my associate's lunch break when I was approached by two FBI agents. They showed me their badges and explained why they would have to wait at this checkpoint. While they were waiting, we were casually talking and of course I was asking them all kinds of questions about their job and what kind of assignments they've experienced. They told me stories about monitoring terrorist activities in the mountains, other criminal activities and possible sightings. They admitted that they get a lot of calls from people that have seen all kinds of sighting through out the mountains.   They said they spend a lot of time tracking strangers, killers and the unknown through the mountains and that they have observed certain groups and a variety of activity for years.

So, how long have I been observing the ways of the world and putting the pieces together, all my life. It took me a while to walk on my own path. I started becoming aware when I was eighteen years old. It seemed that something was not adding up to me. I would wake up thinking, I'm cursed. I did something to God and this is going to be my miserable life! I am different. I am so different, people who are like me are already living a life of that constantly test their inner strength.

As a teenager, and after graduating from high school, it was clear that history taught me that I was born into three different categories of hate. Because we have very strong women in our family who "believe", is why I'm standing here today. My mother was firm while raising us and prayed over us many nights. She taught us to understand who we are, where we came from, and she helped us develop into the people we are. My brother, sister and I only know family.

We have a father who has always been in our lives. Now my mother and his mother had to strong-arm him at first, but as every smart man figures out, he was fighting a loosing battle and he quickly gave in. I have had uncles, aunts, cousins and grandparents, whom not only helped as a part of our support group, but was there through all the growing pains that families go through.

See, I thought every family had the love and support of their family structure when I was young. It was amazing to grow up and realize that everyday life for some people don't consist of the trials and tribulations of trying to raise and protect their children from day-to-day kaos. Some people just hope their children come home alive!

There are people who were not taught how to get up and better themselves so that their children could see an everyday role model. We have heroes right in our homes and at our work places. They are in our communities and our churches. What about the everyday heroes that have the courage to walk to the grocery store with a cane or only their incredible sense of sound to find their way. They are different too you know. That is courage at its highest level! Sometimes you never reach the level of courage you need because you are to scare to be different! You want to be like everyone else because it easier.

Again, we grew up in a country that plastered the white picket fence syndrome all over the TV, in our schools and our communities. It was a mindset that the government said we should try to achieve. They instilled in our minds that this is the American dream! It is 2008 and you have got to be kidding me if you still believe that! Some of you are lost because you don't know what to believe in.

That's why people like me are still writing books about finding the inner you. What do you believe in? How about believing in you! Can we start there? What an amazing concept. You have to be careful, the symptoms and side effects could cause you to be different! Far as I can see, different is a great category to be in. Christ was different. Remember he died so we could live because he saw that we were different. There go those chills again (I rub my right arm with my left hand).

Let me finish telling you what I now know works for me. If I am allowed to wake up, I will go to work on me. I will work on being the best me I can be each day. The days that I fall down, will be my hardest days at work. Because you can ask the highest power for help, but you have to be willing to help yourself.

Think of this, if you were crouched over on the ground and someone laid on your back, you have the weight of you and that person to overcome before you can stand. But, if you both try to stand together, the burden of the person crouched over on the ground, will not be so great.

That's what we ask from the highest power, everyday! God can you give me strength; God can you help me find my way; God can you take this burden from me! When are you going to help yourself! You are supposed to know what you need and when you need it. Did you get up and do your part of helping your situation today, before you started sending an SOS to God!

The words are clear "seek and you shall find;" they don't say, " I'll do all the work, you just rest!" But they do say, "If you believe in me...!" Some of you keep missing the correlation between, "we are made in his likeness and image," and "if you believe in me!" The message keeps coming to you in different ways and from different people, but it's still the same message. We are made in his likeness and image, and "if you believe in me!" If we are made in his likeness and image, then "if you believe in me," becomes, believing in his likeness and image and therefore, I NEED TO BELIEVE IN ME! We have to walk with the belief of God or whatever name you give your highest power! You have to believe in you in order to understand the power of believing!

I Take My Cold Showers

YOU have to be courageous! You have to step out on faith! You have to be different! There go those chills again. So, now you know why I take my cold showers. It's amazing to have lived long enough to truly be able to say, that I have witness something glorious. I can attest to science, religion, and phenomena, which has granted me the passage of acceptance. I accept that I am ME and that I am DIFFERENT!

In my opinion, my mind is a phenomena and depending on the nurturing through out my life, along with what special gifts granted to me at birth by God, it will reveal things to me I cannot explain, I can only experience. My body is a science and is made from the organisms of the earth that it inhabits. It is volatile to its surroundings, evolution of the earth, and the stars and the planetary alignments. These elements added together equal time. That leaves religion.

This is the hardest concept for non-believers to grasp. However, in my opinion, religion is the key to understanding your soul. It is the spirit of how we live, worship and believe. The scriptures tell the stories of those who were plagued with grief and good according to the spirit in which they lived. They reveal the hardship of wrong doers and the blessings of those that helped others with out seeking reward. The scriptures acts as testimonials throughout history that tell us about events, the difference in the paths that were chosen, and the consequences suffered by those that continued to make poor choices. Then there was the extraordinary presence of Jesus Christ. He was a true prophet with the phenomena of premonition.

The people didn't understand phenomena as we understand it today and they didn't like the fact that he was different, so they destroyed the most beautiful gift sent to the human race. But, the courage he exploited, for what he believed, was unforgettable and will never be matched!

Wars were being fault in that era for the same reasons they are being fault now, including religious belief. This is why ordinary people, explorers, scientists, archeologists and a host of others are still interested in following the scriptures and walking on the holy lands where these biblical stories began.

They talk about Abraham and when the belief in an invisible God began. So, can we say that this is when they acknowledged the power of belief? Today we can distinguish some differences in the scriptures as they describe some events as an act of God and others were the evolution of the planet.

What's interesting is how the cycle of life continues to repeat itself as recorded in the bible. It shows that the various cycles of life have a beginning and end.

Who are you in your life cycle? Are you supposed to be a messenger or a leader; are you a shepherd out to help guide others; or an angel of covenant? Your destiny is the path of least resistance! It is as natural as breathing air. Who are we to question destiny? Who are we to question anything? With our luxuries of running water, grocery stores, indoor plumbing and transportation?

I'll say again, in my opinion, there is an energy that surrounds us, it governs us in a way! I can't explain it, I can only experience it! But,

I have found that the more I acknowledge it, the more I experience its wonders.

What's so damn erotic when I think about it, is the fact that I am a messenger and I'm supposed to be right here today! Every time I do what I'm suppose to be doing on this path, I experience goodness and love at its highest level. The beat of my heart races as it fills with unexplainable joy, tears may fill my eyes with out my control, I feel exhilarated then weightless. I'm so high on the feeling that I never want to come down. It's different every time. It's something I can't predict.

WHAT! Y'all need to get your minds right. Some of y'all need Jesus (as I point around the room enjoying the laugher).

PART II

It's Chemistry Baby

WHAT is a journey with out love and companionship? I have met some diverse people and they all had something to share about their culture, family and failed attempts at relationships. Including the one they had with me. Although this bonding ritual has taken some good and bad turns I'm determined to keep learning until I get it right, some one has pity on me or stays around out of spite.

There is so much to learn about yourself when you have been filled with so much knowledge. I continued to work on myself. I wanted to be better at relationship building. I, like so many others, will work on this until I am in the grave. It is so important to not only know how to treat people to increase your social circle, but to also be aware of whom you invite into your circles. Whether it's your social circle, business circle, friend circle or personal space.

How many of us enter into relationships for all the wrong reasons and why can't we get good relationships to last or go in the right direction.

You can't just say it's okay to invite anyone into your life. I don't think we protect or safe guard our personal space as much as we should. With all the craziness in the world today, you should be aware of those entering into your personal space. Don't forget, we have motive! The biggest and first motive on the list is to be in a relationship.

We all want to meet that special someone to share our time and/or life with. I've been dating since I was sixteen and was burnt out on it by eighteen. Dating in my twenties wasn't very serious, but in my thirties it was got better. I should say, I got better at it. I realized in my early twenties that relationships were better then one-night stands or fad dating. I did some things that I wasn't particularly proud of...and No! You are not about to here about the drama of it all in this book. But keep reading all the same. I did have something extraordinary happen to me.

It was Friday and I was glad to have been invited out by some new people. I had put myself in time-out after my last relationship. It's something I do; it allows me to get my bearings again and recoup my thoughts. I don't place blame anymore; it takes two and why torture yourself or the other person. You both know who did what, when and why. So, save yourself some additional grief and start the "move it along" process.

Unfortunately, for some people that means crawl from under one person and crawl on top of another. Yeah...I have never gotten that part. I wanted to at least figure out what I did so I don't take my baggage into the next relationship. But time to heal is essential for me. I take the time to rejuvenate my mind, body and spirit.

I feel it's important to know how to heal myself and to start the process as soon as possible. That's why there is no time to place blame. I find it draining to keep rehashing the same old shit that caused you to be split up in the first place. The blame game becomes a long ass walk down a dark ass street. You're alone and cold! Which pisses you off even more. The next thing you know, you're depressed and drained of energy and for what?

You can't make someone love you the way you want them to love you. It never fails, I say that I'm going to try harder, do better and give more of myself, but it's not working for me. I'm learning as I go and for me, it's a formula of the right kind of person, at the right time in my life and lust just won't do, I must have desire.

Sorry, I can't bend on desire anymore. Lust goes away. Besides that, lust is scary and has been for years. So, those of you who can have relationships for three years or more built on sex, rock on with your bad self.

I know that my mind has to think of you, my heart has to feel inflated from the love I have for you. And whenever I hold you close to me, the energy flowing between us will make your body cling to mine like a magnet. My spirit must be at peace in or out of your presence. Which means that you're participating in this relationship at the same level that I am. How important is that? Well, It's very important.

Hell by the time the sixth month, when you should be switching into another gear for the better, some of us are wondering if we still feel the same way. If the thought of "if" has already reared it's nasty head, then you may want to re-think what you're doing and how your going to do it.

Don't waste people's time with your personal bu#+sh%=. It's not fair to them. Plus, while you're playing with their emotions and wasting their valuable time not knowing what you want or what direction you want or need the relationship to go in, they could be missing the person who does give a damn about them, just for whom they are. So in a sense, your pissing away two peoples' lives while you play let's make my mind up.

That's why I still think dating is very important. Take the time to get to know your mate's wants, needs, ambitions and that inner child that seeks out occasionally and makes you smile.

Don't forget to ask yourself; where you are in your growth cycle and where the other person is in their growth cycle? If you decide to become a couple are you both able to grow together or is one of you not ready to continue growing right now. Before you say, "I can wait for him or her to catch up to me", you should think about this one or two more times.

When your mate doesn't grow at the rate you want them to, a breakup or breakdown in the relationship is waiting around the corner. You are the only person that knows what you can and cannot tolerate. So don't be running to your friends trying to get them to see your side.

You should be working on getting the person your interested in to see your side. Keep in mind that you have to start giving immediately when you start to know someone if you want them to start giving in return.

This is an important door that should swing both ways for you and your person of interest. Whom is the responsible person in the relationship to monitor the door swing. You both should be making it your business to ensure that you both are entering and exiting this door with the mutual agreement that you will let nothing or no one close it on either of you.

I feel that relationships have to be built in our bodies and our minds. There is two parts to this relationship that has to have one common goal to maintain a strong bond. Remember this saying " don't forget the glue"; don't worry, I won't let you forget as you read alone.

If we think about it, the relationship of the minds should be first. It starts out like playing tag. I call you and now it's your turn to call me. You call me back and you ask some very basic questions about me. I like that.

Don't be afraid to talk about you. You should know with out a doubt how to talk about what makes you the person that you are. You need to make sure that you know this person introducing them self to you. After all, this is the person you have to decide if you can build a relationship with.

Now, it's your turn. I want to here some basic characteristics about you while I listen to the person-ality in the way you tell me about you. You've got my attention. I must admit, I want to know more. In order for you to feel comfortable telling me more, I will open the door a little more and tell you this side of me first. Hopefully, you will open the door easily and extend your thoughts as freely as I did.

It's been a couple of days since we've last spoke although we did exchange "hello's" threw our voicemails. I've had time to think about the character of this new personality. My thoughts were pondering likes and dislike of my past conversations with this person. Okay, okay...I'm ready to take another step.

I called but your not available. I leave my work and home schedules on your voicemail so you can call me when you're ready. I'm just letting them know when I most likely will have time to talk for a moment. Which means I've open the door a little more once again. I'm all right with taking the lead here, because I'm interested in knowing more about them.

Ladies, keep in mind that everyone is scared of rejection but if you don't have the nerve to convince him that your still interested, then he may think your not and not take you seriously. Men and women have to be guided by each other through out the getting to know you process and the keep on getting to know you process. Remember that we all continue to grow in relationships. If I'm participating, I will recognize changes in your growth cycle and I hope you recognize the changes in mine.

So, later that evening, my call was returned and I can tell they're smiling on the other end of the phone, which makes me melt like butter as a sweet smile forms on my face and I thank them for leaving the message. I feel they were letting me know they were thinking about me with out being to forward....I get that and I like it. Which is why I totally felt it was my turn to make a move. Yes, I also left a voicemail saying "hello", but my call was in response to their call. Which meant, it was my turn.

I don't know about you all, but I have my own feline approach. I have to check you out from a distance, then I walk your way slowly, while I'm still checking you out. Then eventually I will approach you and check you out up close. I will decide if I want to get to know you better by brushing up against you. Yes, I know I have issues and now I know y'all have issues to;

This fundamental game of tag has been a pleasant way of getting to know my new person. I want to hold your hand but, with words.

I comment on how sweet your smile sounds in your voice and let you know how buttery my smile fell across my face in reaction to the phone vibe. Vibes are great. It's my first contact with your chemistry. The mind vibe is flowing and a little piece of my defensive wall starts to come down.

You all know how it is...after a bad break-up, you may not be dealing with a wall, I may have to be retrieved from the middle of a concrete tunnel with rod iron gates on both ends. We have all been there and some of us more than once or twice.

So I'm feeling okay about the two-way vibe. That's what this is about for me. I want that relationship with your mind. I tell you what's been up in my world since our last conversation. I skip over anything that was dramatic. Not just for them, but for me to. I'm enjoying my mood right now and reflecting on drama can kill a mood faster than Ortho can kill a weed. Don't do it people.

I can tell that you want to keep this vibe going through your questions and answers. We're smiling and sometimes laughing through our fun conversations of what we thought the other was thinking at this point. We know we have to end our call soon but not with out one of us asking when is a good time to call next. This gives us a few more minutes to talk as we hash out our schedules for the next day or so. But it's clear that we both want to make time for the next call.

This is a good thing. Now I get a chance to ponder the last conversation. What questions do I have for them? Was I able to answer them from the conversations I've had thus far or do I need to add these questions to my up coming conversation?

Where will my questions lead? Hopefully to the next level… Do I want to open the door a little more personally or professionally? Think about what is important to know about this person at this point.

What if they have children? I Do. This is a very important part of any relationship.

I had to build a relationship with each child connected to my partner. Do not skip this step or think that it's going to be easy, especially if the child is over five years old. You need to take your time and be diligent.

If this doesn't work for you, don't fake it because you won't last and the relationship will end. We all know men are still notorious for not trying to have a relationship with a woman that has children. But women are just as guilty.

Don't be fooled, there are women doing the same thing it's just the percentage of women that won't date a man with children may be a little lower. Most women have tolerated being around children longer then men; so we know where the behavior comes from. However, women need to stop acting like this is not a fact. I've spoken to a large number of women that just date men for the sex and didn't want a committed relationship because he had joint or primary custody of his children.

In this case, you can have well-mannered children or not, and a woman or man isn't going to stay with you. For those of us that have lived this scenario, we know they don't want the responsibility.

If you were taught responsibility, you may deal with responsibility better then someone that wasn't. There are many levels of responsibility and some of us can handle certain responsibilities more effectively then others.

That all being said, when your pondering what questions to ask this new person that your now feeling good vibes from, make the questions effective to what you need to know and what you want to know about this persons life style. We can determine a lot about how to proceed through the dating process by just asking the right questions at the right time.

This is why jumping into the relationship with the body to soon, can make you forget what the hell you're suppose to know about a person. Now your happy behind is running around in after glow and have convinced yourself "everything will work out find".

Say it with me, "no it won't!" How many times have we said this to ourselves?   Especially women! We are notorious for the "rose colored glasses syndrome". Six months later, when we know damn well that this is not the woman or man we're going to have a future with, we are trying to convince our friends and family that "everything will work out find".

First they look at you crazy. Then they start staying away from you. They know you will eventually see it when you come down from your personal high, that this person doesn't like you, like you like them.

I should know. I knew someone that I dated for three weeks and was reluctant to date them from the start but gave in to being pressured by them. When I said I didn't want to date them any longer, they went into a jealous rage and tried to run me over with their car.

Yes, I had slept with them already and what I thought was casual sex turned out to mean more to them. Needless to say, casual sex is out for me. I don't need to have a set of bridge-stone tires marked across my back to figure that out. Some things should only take one lump up side the head.

For those men that are reading this book, you know why your car got keyed or you went out side and had four flat tires and some of you have been stalked. For women that have done this to men, some of you have been hit, some of your houses have been broken into and others have been stalked.

This is the result of our actions. Not to be confused with "it's all my fault and this is why these things happened to me". I am not saying that at all. What I am saying is that we don't know what makes a person snap! When people don't want to control their emotions and all they want to do is jump the curb with their car and drive over your ass, then that's what they're going to do. I wish tying a bumper to your self could help. But since it won't... I suggest you learn how to "run Forest!"

So I say to you, take all the time you need to get to know someone's mind and how they think. Trust me, a little bit of crazy is in us all if the right trigger is pulled. If you figure out what that trigger is, think of it like a weapon. It's loaded and could do bodily harm.

How do you decide if you can deal with a person that shows you apart of them that you don't like. This is a tough decision for some of us; it does depend on, if it's behavior I can deal with or not. If it's bad or violent behavior, for myself, I'm getting the hell away from them as fast as humanly possible.

I was in another relationship with a person that I loved with all of me. I showed them how much I cared for them by going through a turbulent emotional relationship. I said emotional, right. I thought that I could be there for them while they fault through their emotional decisions and addiction.

I made sure everything was taken care of; the bills, the house and the cars. To only find out later, that I wasn't helping them at all by doing everything. What I did was give them more time to grow in their addiction.

My Sociologist explained to me that people have to learn how to fight their own demons. I tried to support them by suggesting they get professional help but all that did was make them sneak around and lye about being under the influence.

Ultimately, I had to make a decision for me. I left; after ending the relationship I thought that was it. I wasn't around them and therefore I didn't have to deal with their problems. That was not true. I still was going through something. I had to deal with the after effects. When I left, I still loved them very much, still had the separation anxiety and the worry for their well-being. However, my sanity was at stake. I was in love but miserable. That saying "happiness in hell" came to mind.

We need to know when to say, "it's time to go".

Times have surely changed for my generation. We are supportive in our relationships and strong for our family and partners. But... we're not letting them or anyone else drag us in the ground.

I had to be true to who I am as a woman. My inner self said run like hell Gamina! I didn't take but a small suitcase full of clothes and walked, not drove, away.

From that day forward, I said never again! I mean that with every breath I take. It's hard enough to fight your own demons, but to get another adult to understand that you can only do so much to help them fight their demons is an up hill battle.

 Sometimes we get so comfortable in our relationships we think, they won't find out and if they do, they'll forgive me. You just lied to yourself. Yes, people grow and they do things that you hope will pass. But, as I've learned, just because you can try certain things and move on doesn't mean your partner has the same ability.

I was introduced to, addictive personalities by my sociologist. Some of us have addictive behavior and some of us don't. However, if the tendency is available it could be activated.

For me, this is why the dating process works. But after what I've been through, seen and the stories I've heard, we will be dating longer and longer. You all do what works for you, but dating helps me set the pace when I'm getting to know someone. This is not a race. Which is why I referred to the beginning of the dating process is like playing tag. At some point I have to decide to proceed and at some point if I don't feel comfortable about what I'm learning from this new person, I can stop now while it's still in the "getting to know you stage".

Let's say I want to continue to talk to this new person and I'm ready for the answers to my questions.

QUESTION: What do I need from the person in my life and what do I want from the person in my life?

This is a two-part question for me because needs and wants are two different things. I need a person that is independent and respectful, God fearing, trustworthy and philosophical, who doesn't mind being spontaneous from time-to-time, who has passion for culture and creativity and who doesn't mind getting to know my daughter; a people person. A person that understands, I like living well and investing in the financial marketplace and investing my time in people.

I want a person that is not attached to drama, who likes to travel, easy going but full of energy; someone that knows when to be supportive and when to take the lead. That's confident and doesn't have displaced jealousy or envy. Someone, who can deal with my busy life style with out feeling insecure.

When I'm listening to my answers, I'm comparing them to my lifestyle. I've added up the positives and negatives and have decided at this point if I want to date this person long enough to see if they meet some of my wants and needs.

I have asked simple questions to complicated questions.

Did you date your last partner long enough to see if they had good work habits? Do you? Do you know why you like them? Do you know why they like you? Have you asked yourself if they are just filling a void in your life right now? That's an important question that we all need to ask our self.

We don't have to pretend to love or even like someone more then we do if they are just filling a void in our life right now. This allows people to only give and get what they need, if they chose to participate. If they don't, then you know that person isn't willing to deal with you on those terms. But you would be surprised at how many people are okay with it.

I think it's important not to mislead people's emotions. We're human and we don't want to feel stupid in relationships. They are tough enough already. So if you say "I like you, do you want to move in together?"

You may have caught me totally off guard with that question. I'm going to feel like I'm not trying hard enough and this person is really serious or I'm not ready for that type of commitment and should speak up. Don't just move in because you feel bad for the other person.

The truth is painful but it does allow people to adjust their feelings and they have an option to deal with you on your terms or not. If the truth is, your not that serious about a person, you just need some financial help; well, get a roommate damnit! Don't confuse people like that.

We have the Oprah Winfrey Show, the Dr. Phil Show and a host of others that are giving us information on relationships but some of you aren't listening with your good ear. You can't have healthy relationships with out working on trying to have a good relationship.

So, here I am trying to have a good and healthy relationship. I'm holding out for what I think is the right person to come along. As I've grown mentally from my past relationships, what I think is the right person has continued to evolve. I don't think there's a perfect person, let me be clear, but I believe there's a person that fits me indeed.

Not just compatible, because compatibility has different levels as well. There is a person out there that fits me like a glove. That feeling is incredible. It's chemistry baby; you could have a lot going on and still not have chemistry. I have to hold out for all that I know, want, desire, compatibility and chemistry.

I can attest to one of my previous relationships, as chemistry. It was as close to perfect as I've experienced. This was a person of grace, beauty and character. My needs and wants were filled and yet today...I am a single woman. What happened you ask? Well, many things can be encapsulated within your relationship. Everyone handles their emotions differently. What could be minor to me could be something huge for them. In this case, it was indeed more challenging then I could have ever imagined.

Although I had seen and talked to them on a few occasions prior to getting to know them personally, I didn't think I would ever be in a relationship with this person. I did think they were very down to earth and genuine when ever we seen each other at a local shop we visited. We would speak to each other and I would join in the laughter they shared with a friend about the shortcomings of living in Chicago. They both grew up there.

My mother was from there and my grand-mother lived there so my sister, brother and I were there every weekend when we were young.

These occasional visits were getting more interesting for me because they started talking to me more and eventually, it was suggested that we should go to lunch sometime. I felt comfortable going to lunch after months and months of general conversation and they were easy on the eyes. So I did what any woman would do when a well-groomed, attractive person makes a suggestion as such; I exchanged phone numbers and set up a lunch appointment as soon as possible.

That led to some very pleasant phone conversations of getting to know each other. We laughed about the natural comedy that raising children brings to a parents life style. We tried to determine an age when our children will stop calling home for money. I spoke up and said "at least thirty-five". I said, the brakes went out on my car last week and I had to call my father for money. I heard laughter out loud and "you've got to be kidding me. You're a career woman". I replied, "yeah... what's your point?"

I couldn't wait to receive their phone calls. I always went to bed smiling after our conversations. We talked about everything and they could talk about anything and make me smile. I was totally captivated by the way they walked and talked.

Plus I had an added bonus, they were from Chicago and I wanted to finish the rest of my career there because my family lived two hours away. I've worked in Chicago and literally have been in the city every month for one reason or another. I've always wanted to retire there.

Before, we started to get to know each other personally, I had returned from one of my regular trips from Chicago and had decided to start dating someone that lived there because I would be transferring from Denver. So I was happy that everything was going well. I shared this information with them and mentioned how pleased I was about our progress.

I still wanted to know more about this persons character, personality and confidence and this would require spending more time together. Which meant I had to make time for more lunches, dinners, breakfasts and events. A holiday came and we exchanged gifts. Some months had pasted and finally it was time to plan a weekend together. We both had a great time and that's all I'm admitting to you all.

We were both engaged in this new relationship that continued to blossom into something wonderful. As our relationship grew we had to also grow our relationship with our children. This part started out a little rough for us because their seventeen yr old daughter wasn't happy about this relationship and didn't approve.

She was in her last year of high school and was planning to go to college. She wanted to finish high school with her friends. She didn't want to move with us at first. She was given a couple of options but she eventually chose to live with us. Of course we had to be persuasive. She and I were still getting to know each other and I wanted her to be comfortable.

My daughter was just being selfish and didn't want me to be with anyone that would take time from her.

Our daughters were also getting to know each other. My daughter was five so she was pleased that she could stay up with the teenagers and watch them braid or curl each other's hair.

We continued to have a growing relationship that led to us moving into together.   We bought a house and remodeled it. While landscaping the yard I managed to crash their car with half a tree that I was cutting down. Yes, I'm a home improvement person. It just goes to show you that we can take home improving to damn far. It was a very expensive lesson in many ways. We replaced the car but the experience haunted me for a while. This was the first test of true forgiveness. Our relationship was able to with stand my disaster.

We bought a second house and rented out the first house. Life for us continued to grow in the right direction. My company was starting to make a lot of internal changes that would affect me transferring with the company. As a result of these changes, It was time to make my move with the company. I went home and discussed this with my partner. Our teenage daughter was attending college on the east cost. My daughter was nine and could travel on a plane with an airlines escort. Both of our parents lived in the mid west. Their parents lived in Chicago and mind in Michigan.

I thought this was going to be easy but it wasn't. This is when I admitted to myself that my partner wasn't quite okay with moving to Chicago. Keep in mind that I'm the one that kept bringing it up.

I thought we were torn between each other's preference to live in one part of the country or the other. But, it was my preference to move. I have my path of destiny and they had their life style of happiness. Our lives were challenged with something different than our love for each other and we recognized this crossroad and tried to accommodate each other. But, it still was at the others expense.

Don't get me wrong; I know I was truly blessed. However, I was running along my path before I met them and they were happy living in Denver before I came along. I tried to bend and so did they. But, ultimately we had some very important decisions to make. I knew I was going to be here in Chicago today. Although I kept bringing up moving here my partner has always wanted to stay in Denver or move some where like Denver.

However I thought because our life style together was so loving and prosperous, we could work this out. But, that's not what we did. We kept trying to do something other then move to Chicago. This was not easy for us. I didn't want to understand how I could be happy and sad at this point in my life. I could have my life style anywhere but couldn't have the growth in my double career in Denver. I apparently couldn't have this person in my life if I were to move to Chicago. But everything in me was screaming; "it's time for me to go in order to keep moving forward".

I had already started networking with my future peers on the East coast. I accepted a promotional transfer to get to the next level because we agreed that we would try Houston, TX. At the last minute my company denied the transfer because another manager was displaced in Dallas that was already in that position. So I signed up for a transfer to Montgomery, NY, and I interview for a position in Ohio.   As long as it was in the Midwest or East coast I would be able to maintain my double career. My other investment career is in property and I could buy property anywhere. My book writing, music and film career was on the rise and my network was in Chicago and New York.

I thought for some reason that things couldn't get any better for me and the bottom fell from under my feet. My transfer to Chicago was approved.

You have to learn how to pull up your big girl panties and make some very tough decisions in your life. I am a very driven person. It's in my blood and my heritage. I can't apologize for who I am. It's not up to me to make decisions about partner's happiness I can only be apart of making them happy.

This is where growing together in some commonality is important. I missed something here and when I realized that they were not going to be happy moving to Chicago. I questioned my decision, again and again, I swallowed, I cried, I screamed, I walked around in a daze for a few weeks and I left.

I wouldn't have been happy staying in Denver. I was ready to go before I met my partner. I stayed because I met them. So, for me, I was in a better position leaving Denver now then I was previously. I was on top of the world and it had a price tag.

It was inconsiderate of me to think just because I was in a good relationship, that my partner thought it was good enough to move out of their comfort zone.

I realize that even after being with someone eight years you have to understand a lot about your self. You can be all that and you can still be missing some key ingredients in your relationship. You may have to look at your self over and over again in that mirror and forgive your self for the decisions you've made. They may not have been perfect, but it was the best decision you could make at that time in your life.

Sometimes it's going to hurt like hell, but you still have to stand tall and step out on faith. Time will tell the story. I say again, you may or may not like it sometimes, but learn how to deal with your good decisions as well as your bad decisions. You are still making a decision that affects your life. Just because you're in a relationship doesn't mean that you're going to see things the same way all the time. But make sure you don't miss the big decisions that are relationship breaking.

I told you that I have to analyze my part in my broken relationships. I forgot an ingredient; it was the glue. What is the glue you ask? The glue is the common bond that keeps you and your partner connected in the relationship. It is the clarity in your communication, the direction of your relationship, being on the same page at the same time about your children, who is in the lead and who is the back up support for the next six months and managing the finances of the house hold. This is after love, respect and honoring your relationship.

There is so much more to do to maintain your relationship so you can keep your relationship.

Someone in the relationship has to keep up with the glue. In most relationships, this position is held by the woman; a.k.a. Home Administrator. She becomes the all "seeing eye" of the past; "we're not going back down that road again"; the present; "be ready at 4:00 so I can drop you off and pick up your sister"; the future; "we should have twenty-five dollars taken out of our checks each pay period and put into a savings account" she can be the Captain of the ship.

She is to be respected and never under estimated. A woman can be many things in a relationship; But most of all, she is a woman first. She can grow a relationship with her nurturing skills or leave you to fin for your self if you don't respect her.

That's why the beginning of a relationship should at least have some substance. You're just trying to gauge something about this new person that tells you it's okay to go to the next level while you continue to get to know them. This is still minimal to what you still have to learn about them. But they should have shown you something in your list of needs and wants.

So here I am trying this again

I've decided that I want to spend time with them in my environment. We went out together and now we're back at my place and I have more questions. What's different about these questions? I can listen to what's being said while I look at the expression in their eyes. If my ears are listening and my eyes are convinced, then I can believe this person is true to what their saying at the moment.

Now, I want to see their environment to confirm their personality. Okay, I also want to make sure they have their own place these days along with a job and a car. It shows responsibility. But, I'm looking for something more. I look for a persons flavor for life. Because at this point you have the good vibes and the warm and fuzzies; you want intimacy.

The relationship of the body is important. But we all know that you can teach someone how to please you if we like the way they treat you. This part of the relationship can be good or bad. However, if the conversation has been strong then making love will be anticipated. Therefore, it will be intense. We can get lost in our pleasures and that's okay. But, I can't base my entire relationship on having a good sex partner. I feel women can struggle with this because some of us equate physical love with love of the heart and mind. Please tell me you know the difference and if you don't, there is a difference.

When I love a persons mind and spirit, making love to them is more intense. I'm not just talking about the anticipation of making love for the first time. It's the passion that you have through out your relationship for each other.

Don't forget about the glue that keeps the bond connected between the relationships of the mind and the body.

When your ready to move further with this new person in your life, don't forget to let them continue to grow into the person they said they were when you met them.

As for me, I'm going to chill back for a while and be me. I have more to come in my life and would like to meet the person in my thoughts. This idea person has the missing ingredient that I need in my formula to flourish. Could this person that's missing in my life be me?

Since I've Met You

ON my journey, a person crossed math path that was beautiful inside. They were very pleasant to talk to but with drawn from the world. You can't see it at first but if your in the presence you feel it radiating from them. Our encounters left me wondering. This chapter bares my thoughts of what they left behind.

Since I've met you, I recognize this formula is very real and this person is out there. How did you come from somewhere in my mind? My eyes were in disbelief as my ears listened to you speak to me. We exchange small talk but my smile told a story of it's own. It's been some time since I've truly wanted the pleasure of sitting in a cozy atmosphere, sharing a glass of ice wine while having a good conversation with someone. A good conversation is like making love to the mind. Don't ever past up an opportunity to talk to someone your interested in; the question is, when will I have my chance again?

Who are you? Just like that, from somewhere you came. Are you truly a reflection of my thoughts?

You are so blessed to be who you are right now. You are grasping a new side of life. Your life started out slow but graduated into something wonderful. Some of your days are truly scary and you don't know if your coming or going sometimes but the key is to find a way to continue being yourself amongst all the glory and the madness. That is the hard part as well. But to be successful, all would envy your true inter beauty.

I have to tell you a story. I find it impossible to have met someone like you at this time in my life. It's true, you resemble someone of great importance.

I have thought of you often. Wondering what your thoughts are about family. Not just the obvious, but what do you look for in that someone who could be a positive addition to your life.

What would make you smile everyday when you came home? Is it knowing that person will be home to you and all they stand for is to do better for your family and them self so you could be proud that you let them in your life. For some of us, it's all about family.

Being able to share your life with people who care about you for caring about them. It's a bond that can't be broken. A strong family doesn't leave room for straying because they know that the love and support they've grown accustom to will be there each and every time.

Is that someone there to hold you up when you are tired but still have more to do before you can rest? Will they come to where you are just to comfort you or talk to you on the phone until you fall asleep from the reassuring sound of their voice?

Can I drive you to where you're going so you can rest your mind for a little while longer while I play some of your favorite songs? If you enjoy music, sometimes your favorite song is in tune with what you are about to do. I'm a fan of good lyrics unless I'm listening to jazz. I like a mean sax and trumpet rhythmically playing to the smooth sound of jazz at the end my day.

It helps me look forward to that hot shower. While the hot water is running down my 5'9" frame, my body becomes relaxed and my mind fills with thoughts of you.

I can't wait to lye down next to you and feel the warmth of your body next to me. I can't wait to kiss you good night or make you smile one more time before we fall asleep and I'm ready to give you as much love as you need when your ready. Just simply lay your body on top of mine.

 If there is a need in your house, let me know and I will help you fill it.

What do you do to achieve peace of mind? Is there such a place for you? Do you take your self on long drives like I do, that includes scenery or continuous views of the lake depending on what I need to find solitude that day?

Does the sun shining and the sky being blue lift your spirits like they do mine?

Did you know that I think it's perfectly okay to take a moment from time to time, just for your self? There is peace in doing so; I've become to expect it of myself and not feel that I'm being selfish.

 See, I trust me to do the right thing for myself and my family, even if I'm by myself. Just because that's what I need at that moment doesn't make it an opportunity to do the wrong thing. I use time to myself to sort through my future plans or analyze important decisions. When you have a family, your decisions affect them.

You have to make the best decision you can make at that time with consideration of their future. Then I go home and share my thoughts with them and ask their opinions.

When I need to be with the person I love in complete solitude. I will ask you to pencil me in for a special day of TLC. Surprises are okay except when a need has to be met. This day could include a secluded spot filled with a little bit of what you like and a little bit of what I like. It will have the comfort we are accustomed to at home and something about it that makes it one of our favorite spots to visit because this is the mood we want filled right now.

Keep in mind that if you can't get away right now to enjoy that long drive in the sunshine, then take a long bubble bath surrounded by candles and sip on a glass of chilled wine while listening to eclectic music in the back ground; just for you. We work so hard at maintaining and getting ahead in life we forget to take time for ourselves periodically, not just once a year at vacation time. It's too important to rejuvenate yourself and your spirit.

Some people don't understand self-healing. You can't be good to anyone else if you're not good to yourself. It's funny how people just want and take from you then expect you to be readily available. It just doesn't work that way most of the time. You can't be available to everyone all the time; it's just not possible. You start thinking "take a number and get in line please".

So tell me, do you just like to be held from time to time? Do you have those moments where you just want to collapse into the arms of the person you love? It's not a weakness in your independence, but a test of your self will to let go just for a moment and be caught by someone special. I find these moments are difficult to admit but very necessary.

If the person in your life is paying attention, they'll be by your side when this need arises and be all to willing to let you rest your head on their chest while they lye back and hold you close to them. Having the arms of someone special wrapped around you is like being covered by a warm blanket; don't you agree?

Can you believe the vibe you feel when you cross the path of some people. You feel like you've met them before; or you feel like you've known them for years and you know you just met them thirty minutes ago. It's a feeling we can't describe any other way.

Let me say, you have moved me. You literally moved me from one place to another with out knowing. You've elevated me and I don't know anything about you except your smile is picturesque and your energy is very moving. You've touched a thought in my mind that was buried deep in my spirit. It's protected so it can't be tarnished. Some how you've awaken that thought and I've been in a different place every since I've met you.

I've asked my self over and over again. How can a stranger turn on light within me? Well God is funny like that. He will move you in the direction you're suppose to travel in one-way or another.

So, never say never right? Where there is a will he will make a way; you'll be shocked but elated. Sometimes that means he has to use the very thing to get your attention that you might not think will be used against you. Trust me, I'm not complaining, I'm explaining.

I've been told, that I've created this same feeling in others by so many people. This is the second time it's happened to me. I'm so taken by the events that have occurred, I can only describe them as blessings.

So I figured I would let everyone know. That once again I've experienced God's graces in an amazing way. You crossing my path was no accident. It's timing. Although I don't know when they will cross again, it only takes one crossing to affect someone. I was hiding, on purpose of course, but hiding all the same. Not in a cowardly way. I just wanted to be left alone for a while why I buried my self in my work. Obviously, I can be found.

Now that I'm not hiding I'm still buried in my work but some clarity about by direction has been added. I wanted to know if I was going the right way and now I know the answer is yes; I'll say it again, "I believe that things do happen for a reason". If you're patient and aware, the reason will reveal itself to you.

You know that saying, "it was right in front of your face?" Well if you don't know what you're looking for how will you recognize it? Sometimes what is good for us and what we think is good for us is two different things. It's like trying to make a want into a need. Don't do it you all.

I now believe that the most lasting relationships happen naturally with out any pre-drama. Forcing someone to be attached to you by getting pregnant is not the answer or the way. Like I said, the truth is painful but it will give you back your options. Don't waste yourself on someone who doesn't care when there are plenty of people who do. Why be treated like a doormat when you can be treated like Queen or a King.

So has anyone showed you how much you are appreciated lately? Have they brought you breakfast in bed and thanked you for just being you? Have they shown you nothing but unconditional love? Have they massaged your back because you said it ached a little today? Have they rubbed your feet because they noticed you trying to rub them when every woman knows it's best to have someone do it for you?

To me unconditional love means; just because you need me today and even if you don't, I'm here for you. You shouldn't have to ask someone to care if they love you. They should recognize the signs and fill in the blanks when necessary. I believe in participating in a relationship and not waiting for someone to ask me to do something that's helpful.

You know the saying, "do on to others as you would have them do on to you". Trust me on this if you continue to show your mate affection and gratitude and they don't return it, stop doing it and watch their response. They will miss the affection and when they ask why you don't do that anymore or act like it's an expectation, please explain the virtues of sharing something that feels good. Remind them; do they think you lavish them with warmth and affection just for them to enjoy or are they so selfish as to think that you don't want them to return the same warmth and affection!

Don't take things for granted. That's when you leave the front door open to your most prized possessions, your loved ones. It can't be said enough, what one person won't do, another will do.

Where You Are Going

KNOWING who you are and where you are going is so important in your life. It only seems logical you should know these two components to guide the selection of a partner in your life or anyone you invite into your life for that matter. But your partner and/or soul mate as we have learned to identify our significant other as, is a very important role to be filled in your life. There is no such thing as, he or she will do for the next two to three years.

I didn't think we thought about relationships as a temporary position that needed to be filled. But we do. We live in a disposable economy and therefore this concept is okay for people. We've already established the fact that relationships don't last forever. Now we know that people accept temporary relationships. So where does that leave falling in love genuinely? Where do we go from here?

Falling in love is not a convenience for me. I do believe there are different degrees of love. But in relationships, there should be love. I think we confuse like with love. I have to like you first before I drift into loving you. I need it to be a natural flow from one stage to the other. This is why I still believe in dating. It is the foreplay that leads to love.

I have to paste the excitement within me as I work through my day. I have to concentrate more to make sure that the overwhelming feeling of like doesn't make me forget to do something at work. So I pull it all together inside my business suit and hope the hell that people can tell something is different about me. But don't ask, I don't kiss and tell. I'm not trying to help them with their daily fantasies, I'm trying to enjoy mine.

I try not to clock watch so I don't wear one anymore. There's to many devices surrounding me at any given moment with the time of day. I remain cool as a light breeze on a fall afternoon and let my day progress as it should. Some days I'm so busy I don't take lunch, I just take a few breaks to replenish my energy and get out of there.

But when I'm dating, or in a relationship, there's things to do on my breaks and lunches outside of the usual bill paying, setting up a service appointment for the car, or cursing out my credit card company. Such as making dinner reservations, purchasing tickets for an event, sending flowers or making a call to just say "hello and I can't wait to see you later".

That's always my favorite part of the day. Going home to my loved ones. I have this thought process that makes me feel very good when I work first and play second. I work hard so I can play hard in an easy way. I like to lavish my loved ones with quality time. That time can be spent doing what they want whether it cost money or not.

Sometimes it's finally being able to have the day off together so we can go shopping to decorate a room in the house. Add having lunch together at one of our favorite restaurants and the closeness of being in the same car together touching each others faces, kisses at red lights and feeling on each other to help stimulate our mood for later. We can catch up on what plans we want to make for up coming events that we want to attend and the happenings with our parents or siblings.

As the back of my hand is being caressed and my hair is enjoying the periodic stroke of your fingertips on the way home, all I can think about is the intimacy that will follow.

The taste of wine lingering on your tongue increases the passion in my kiss as I enjoy a double taste of you while you undress me.

As soon as I slide your pants past your but and help you with your shirt off, I will get my wish of feeling your body next to mine even sooner. I love to look in your eyes when you're kissing me. It ensures me that I am a part of your fantasy right now. My job is to stay a part of each moment and not let your mind drift elsewhere for pleasure while I have you wrapped around me.

Simple pleasures can still be enjoyed; it's definitely in the touch of the person your dealing with. They would need to give a damn about pleasing your body and your mind. Pleasure will respond to pleasure. And my mind is always open to be taught. How can you tell if you were a good teacher unless your student can practice? You never know how much homework they may require to perfect their new skills.

So, what about you; do you know what truly gives you pleasure?

What defines what you enjoy most? Can you tell me? I will be careful to stop when you say stop. When you say go I will go, and when you say more I will give as much as you can stand.

There is so much to learn about a person that it seems we never really know them completely because we're always growing. People don't stay in relationships long enough to know more than the basic characteristics about their partner. I think we become too comfortable in relationships and therefore we don't try as much to maintain that closeness that makes us still feel wanted.

It takes effort. But the saying is still true; "you get out of a relationship what you put into a relationship." For those of you that wonder why your partner doesn't do the same things anymore, look in the mirror.

My intentions are not to let stagnation into my relationship. I make a conscious effort to communicate about all aspects of my relationship. Yes, although I have a busy career, I still make this possible. I have found that some people can deal with my busyness and some can't.

Which is why it's so important to know yourself so you can identify the right partner. I figured this out the hard way. But trust me it makes sense. You can't identify what you haven't experienced. I had to live through my broken relationships in order to know why certain people's characteristics aren't compatible to mind. That's okay, I just know to take more time to evaluate a person for more compatible traits. It helps but it's not the cure all; there still is self-identity.

Don't be afraid to be yourself. That becomes the billboard to who you are. Stand tall and be proud of the person looking back at you in the mirror. Take a deep breath and introduce you to your self.

A Message To My Readers

KEEP in mind that there will always be authors, story-tellers and others finding new and innovative ways through books, movies, media and seminars to get you to understand you are a part of something great! So, don't sell yourself short! You never know what destiny has in store for you! But as sure as the time of your birth was stamped by the heavens, so was your destiny! Wake up and walk on that path! You'll be absolutely amazed!

Thank you for reading this book.

Please come and join me at book signings or for live

video taped seminars in your city.

www.ingramcontent.com/pod-product-compliance
Lightning Source LLC
Chambersburg PA
CBHW061344160726
47995CB00001B/171